Catholic WORD Games

Mary Bartlett

Liguori
ONE LIGUORI DRIVE
LIGUORI MO 63057-9999

Imprimi Potest:
Thomas D. Picton, CSsR
Provincial, Denver Province
The Redemptorists

ISBN 978-0-7648-1430-3
Library of Congress Number: 2006933878

© 2006, Gabriel Publications
Printed in the United States of America
14 13 12 11 / 7 6 5 4

This book was previously published by Gabriel Publications under the title *Word Games for Catholics,* © 2001.

Liguori Publications, a nonprofit corporation, is an apostolate of the Redemptorists. To learn more about the Redemptorists, visit Redemptorists.com.

To order, call 800-325-9521
www.liguori.org

CONTENTS

CROSSWORDS

WORD SEARCH PUZZLES

GAMES

SOLUTIONS

THE HEART OF CATHOLICISM

ACROSS

4 Roman governor who condemned Jesus
5 Number of gospels
7 First diocese of America
8 You should hark when these kinds of angels sing
12 Place where you find nuns
14 Primary symbol of baptism
15 Head of a diocese
17 Mother of Jesus
20 New Testament book
21 Teaching story told by Jesus
24 He heads an abbey
26 Notre Dame "Fighting _____"
27 Epistle
28 Number of apostles
29 Chief apostle
31 What Jesus turned water into at Cana
32 Eternal union with God
34 Local church community
35 Catholic actor, star of *The West Wing*
40 Temple city
43 Sacrament that makes us a member of the Church
44 Laying on of _____
45 Ordained ministers
47 Celestial being
49 What we call a passage from the Bible
50 Promises
51 Number of sacraments
54 What we call the week before Easter
55 A sacrament is an outward _____
56 Permanent _____
59 Formerly Saul
60 Disciple chosen by Jesus
61 Saintly companion of Francis

DOWN

1 Mission road, *El _____ Real*
2 Where the pope resides
3 Dominicans and Franciscans
6 He shares in the holy orders of his bishop
9 A bishop heads this
10 First gospel
11 Priest, ____, king
13 Reformation era council
16 Our Lady of _____
18 "I am who I am" (Ex 3:14)
19 Leader of the Catholic Church
22 Saint of Lima
23 Nativity
25 First Catholic President of the U.S.
28 Saint of Avila
29 Old Testament liturgical song
30 Doctrine that states God is Father, Son, and Holy Spirit
33 Central sacrament
35 Saint Elizabeth _____
36 Day we celebrate the resurrection
37 First book of the Bible
38 Helps the pope to administer the world-wide Church
39 Sacrament of holy _____
41 Prefix that designates the largest diocese in a province
42 Cardinals _____ the pope
43 Scripture
46 Catholic actor, Mel _____
47 Hometown of Saint Francis
48 "Good news"
52 Where the Holy Family fled to escape Herod
53 Non-ordained members of the Church
54 Nickname for Catholic Georgetown University
57 _____ City
58 He parted the Red Sea

Answers on page 71

OLD TESTAMENT BOOKS

See if you can fill in the missing letters for the books of the Old Testament below.
All missing letters are consonants.

1   __ O __ __ O __ __ O __ O __ O __

2   __ E __ O __ __ __ A __ __ A __ E   E __

3   I __ A   I   A __

4   __ __ A __ __ __

5   __ I __ A __ __

6   __ E __ E __ I __

7   __ O __ __ U   A

8   A __ O __

9   __ E __ __ A __ I   A __

10 __ I __ __ __ __ I __ __ __

11 __ E __ E __ I   A __

12 E __ O __ U __

13 E __ __ A

14 __ I __ A __

15 __ I __ __ __ __ A __ U   E __

16 E __ __ __ E __

17 __ A __ U __ __

18 __ O   E __

19 E __ E __ I   E __

20 __ E   U __ E __ O __ O __ __

21 __ __ O __ E __ __ __

22 E __ __ __ E __ I   A __ __ E __

23 __ A __ A __ __ U __

24 __ E __ I __ I __ U __

25 __ U __ __

Answers on page 93

26 __ O __

27 __ O __ I __

28 __ A __ A __ __ I

29 __ E __ O __ __ __ A __ U E __

30 __ U I __ __ __

31 __ A __ I E __

32 __ U __ __ E __ __

33 __ E __ O __ __ __ I __ __ __

34 __ U __ __ E __

35 __ I __ __ __ __ __ __ O __ I __ __ E __

36 __ E __ E __ I A __

37 __ O __ E A

38 __ I __ __ __ __ A __ __ A __ E E __

39 __ O __ A __

40 __ E __ O __ __ __ __ __ O __ I __ __ E __

41 __ A __ E __ __ A __ I O __ __

42 O __ A __ I A __

43 __ A __ U __

44 __ A __ __ A I

45 __ E __ __ A __ I A __

Answers on page 93

JUGGLED GEOGRAPHY

John's teacher wants the class to learn New Testament places. She has mixed up the names of New Testament cities, bodies of water, and other sites. Can you help John do his homework and straighten out these mixed-up places?

1   Jordan Philippi   _____

2   Sea to Jericho   _____

3   Herod's Room   _____

4   Pool of the Skull   _____

5   Garden of Bethsaida   _____

6   Road of Galilee   _____

7   Upper Temple   _____

8   Dead River   _____

9   Place at Gethsemane   _____

10 Caesarea Sea   _____

Answers on page 93

WORD BUILDER NO. 1

TRANSCENDENT

Form all the four- and five-letter words you can by using only the letters in the word **TRANSCENDENT**. You may use a letter more than once in a word only if it appears more than once in **TRANSCENDENT**. Words beginning with capital letters, plurals, contractions, and hyphenated, slang, poetic, and foreign words are not allowed. Check our list of four- and five-letter words.

Answers on page 93

U.S. BASILICAS

A basilica is a church so designated because of its antiquity, dignity, historical importance, or significance as a center of worship.

ALABAMA

ARIZONA

CALIFORNIA

COLORADO

FLORIDA

GUAM

ILLINOIS

INDIANA

IOWA

KENTUCKY

LOUISIANA

MARYLAND

MASSACHUSETTS

MICHIGAN

MINNESOTA

O	A	N	A	I	D	N	I	S	N	O	C	S	I	W
N	G	U	A	M	I	C	H	I	G	A	N	M	Y	C
L	O	U	I	S	I	A	N	A	L	D	A	P	P	R
C	C	D	N	O	T	G	N	I	H	S	A	W	A	Y
E	I	N	W	M	L	M	F	N	S	H	I	I	T	F
N	R	A	N	I	L	O	R	A	C	H	T	R	O	N
I	O	L	W	N	R	I	C	V	O	Y	M	U	K	E
L	T	Y	K	N	L	H	D	L	L	K	B	O	A	W
L	R	R	I	E	U	O	A	Y	O	C	F	S	D	J
I	E	A	C	S	M	X	R	S	R	U	L	S	H	E
N	U	M	E	O	F	H	I	N	A	T	O	I	T	R
O	P	T	Z	I	M	Z	N	D	N	R	M	R	S
I	T	E	X	A	S	D	O	E	O	E	I	W	O	E
S	K	R	O	Y	W	E	N	P	P	K	D	C	N	Y
V	I	R	G	I	N	I	A	L	A	B	A	M	A	I

MISSOURI   NORTH DAKOTA   TEXAS

NEW JERSEY   OHIO   VIRGINIA

NEW YORK   PENNSYLVANIA   WASHINGTON, D.C.

NORTH CAROLINA   PUERTO RICO   WISCONSIN

Answers on page 75

CROSSWORD PUZZLE NO. 2

ACROSS

1 Biblical victim of fratricide
5 Container for hosts
12 Fog
13 Very skilled person
14 "To be," to Cicero
15 River in central Switzerland
16 Nephew of Abraham
17 Zoological suffix
18 Darken
20 Bathing suit top
21 New Testament epistle (abbr.)
22 Biblical hunter
24 Communion plate
27 Electrically charged atom
28 Follower suffix
29 Minor prophet
30 Religious instruction classes (abbr.)
31 Heath
32 Eve was created from a _____ of a man
33 Definite article
34 Religious ceremonies
35 Hebrew word for "Lord"
37 Resinous deposit
38 Tribe of Israel
39 An archangel
43 Trademark
45 Wreath of flowers
46 Jesus' word for the Father
47 Cheese
48 "For as often as you _____ this bread…" (1 Cor 11:26)
49 "___ lema sabachthani?" (Mk 15:34)
50 Free from germs
51 What you sometimes do with a hand

DOWN

1 Evil king of Israel
2 False god of the Old Testament
3 Old Testament leader of the Restoration
4 Blood suckers
5 One of Joshua's spies
6 Holy image
7 Wager
8 Outfit for war again
9 Judas _____
10 Exploit
11 Wanders
19 Understanding
20 Storage container
22 Land to which the murderer of 1A went
23 A Native American tribe
24 Jesus used these to teach
25 Among
26 Sled
27 Finish the cake
30 ___-Rho
31 Another like 39A
33 A bit
34 Knock vigorously
36 Mother-in-law of Ruth
37 Nonclergy
39 Kind of admiral
40 Capable
41 Black
42 "…and ___ him in a manger…" (Lk 2:7)
44 Room in a harem
45 Meadow

Answers on page 72

APOSTLES & DISCIPLES

Apostles were the handpicked followers of Jesus. Disciples were simply followers of Jesus. So an apostle is a disciple, but a disciple is not necessarily an apostle!

ANDREW

BARNABAS

BARTHOLOMEW

DIDYMUS

JAMES THE GREATER

JAMES THE LESS

JUDAS ISCARIOT

JUDE

LAZARUS

MARTHA

MARY MAGDALENE

MATTHEW

MATTHIAS

NATHANAEL

PAUL

PETER

PHILIP

SIMON

THADDAEUS

THOMAS

J	E	O	M	L	U	A	P	D	A	P	E	T	E	R	J
U	S	V	X	A	M	Q	D	Q	J	H	A	J	E	N	A
D	O	H	K	X	R	A	H	O	J	C	T	T	T	A	M
E	P	W	N	X	N	Y	M	S	M	T	A	R	H	F	E
O	D	S	N	E	S	Q	M	X	B	E	U	W	A	B	S
J	U	D	A	S	I	S	C	A	R	I	O	T	A	M	T
S	P	T	U	Z	H	S	Q	G	G	U	E	R	J	S	H
A	I	Q	T	S	I	W	E	U	M	D	T	Z	U	F	E
I	L	E	A	N	A	H	T	A	N	H	A	E	Y	S	L
H	I	A	Q	J	T	B	T	N	O	W	A	L	A	O	E
T	H	P	Z	S	W	T	A	L	S	D	D	M	E	D	S
T	P	A	E	A	H	R	O	N	D	I	O	T	K	N	S
A	Z	M	M	E	R	M	L	A	R	H	M	N	C	J	E
M	A	A	W	F	E	U	H	R	T	A	K	O	G	F	X
J	R	N	B	W	U	T	S	Z	S	T	B	Y	N	V	F
Y	D	I	D	Y	M	U	S	W	E	R	D	N	A	Q	K

Answers on page 75

BROTHER SUN, SISTER MOON

Saint Francis of Assisi is said by many to be the greatest spiritualist that Europe has ever produced. Many religious orders follow the rule and example of Francis.

ANIMALS   BERNARDONE   ACTION   ECOLOGY   FRANCISCANS

BEGGING   BROTHER SUN   CLARE   EUROPE   INNOCENT III

ORDER   CATHOLIC   CRECHE   FOUNDER   ITALY

MENDICANT

MIDDLE AGES

MINISTRY

PEACE

POOR

PREACHING

RULE

SAN DAMIANO

SPIRITUAL

STIGMATA

THIRTEENTH CENTURY

```
B E G K E L X F A Y J I M Z K A P T
L R W N H P E B R Y I K I E D U H T
A A O V I P O T K I D S D Z F I E L
U L O T K H S R T C A S D G R Y C S
T C X E H I C N U N G Y L T A R O N
I X E K N E E A D E L P E A C E L A
R P K I E C R A E A Z E A R D H O C
I E M K O D M S T R N N G U Y G G S
P C D N G I X I U T P H E L U D Y I
S A N R A T G M H N K C S E H K X C
E I N N O I T C A C I L O H T A C N
M U O I A G E T N A C I D N E M F A
Z P Y L M N N P R E W F Y P R O H R
E Y C B T A D I O K X I Q N U D H F
X H E U E N L X G O F R K N H Z X I
F S R N D O H S H G R B D W R I H A
U Y S T I G M A T A E E H C E R C M
B E R N A R D O N E R B S J F C G V
```

Answers on page 75

WHICH IS IT?

The object of this puzzle is to fill in the blanks below by choosing the correct answer to each of the following questions. The answer will tell you what letter to enter into which blank space below. If you answer the questions correctly, a gospel proclamation will be spelled out.

$$\overline{}\ \overline{}\ \overline{}\ \overline{}\ \overline{}\ \overline{}\ \overline{}\ \overline{}\ \overline{}$$
$$1 \quad 2 \quad 3 \quad 4 \quad 5 \quad 6 \quad 7 \quad 8 \quad 9$$

1   If Pentecost is fifty days after Easter, then 4 is S. If it is forty, then 4 is T.

2   If the wise men's visit is celebrated on Epiphany, then 9 is N. If it is celebrated on the feast of Christ the King, then 9 is R.

3   If there are seven holy days in the United States, then 7 is N. If there are six, then 7 is S.

4   If the feast day of Saint Joseph is March 17, then 2 is A. If it is March 19, then 2 is E.

5   If the Immaculate Conception refers to Jesus' conception, then 1 is I. If it refers to Mary's, then 1 is H.

6   If the apostle Peter's brother is Andrew, then 5 is R. If his brother is James, then 5 is P.

7   If Jesus cured Peter's mother, then 3 is A. If he cured Peter's mother-in-law, then 3 is I.

8   If Teresa of Avila is a doctor of the Church, then 6 is I. If she is not, then 6 is U.

9   If the first council of the Church was the Council of Jerusalem, then 8 is E. If it was the Council of Nicaea, then 8 is A.

Answers on page 93

TITLES USED IN HOLY ORDERS

Members of the clergy are known by many different titles. These titles designate the responsibilities of the person. How many can you identify?

ABBOT

BISHOP

CELEBRANT

CHANCELLOR

CHAPLAIN

CLERGY

CURATE

DEACON

DOM

FATHER

JUDICIAL VICAR

MINISTER

MONSIGNOR

PARSON

PASTOR

PREACHER

PRELATE

PRESBYTER

PRESIDER   RECTOR

PRIEST   REVEREND

PROVINCIAL   SUPERIOR

J	D	D	B	C	D	N	E	R	E	V	E	R	R
R	U	R	Z	H	P	R	E	L	A	T	E	E	T
O	W	D	O	A	P	A	R	S	O	N	H	P	P
I	B	P	I	N	P	A	B	B	O	T	N	R	N
R	I	A	R	C	G	R	Y	H	A	N	O	E	R
E	S	S	O	E	I	I	E	F	I	V	C	S	E
P	H	T	T	L	C	A	S	A	I	E	A	I	T
U	O	O	C	L	X	A	L	N	C	D	E	D	Y
S	P	R	E	O	O	P	C	V	O	H	D	E	B
E	B	R	R	A	I	P	M	I	M	E	R	S
B	G	L	B	H	A	E	P	Y	I	C	L	R	E
Y	Z	Q	C	L	E	T	A	R	U	C	A	X	R
T	N	A	R	B	E	L	E	C	Y	X	U	R	P
T	S	E	I	R	P	M	I	N	I	S	T	E	R

Answers on page 75

THE CROSS

Over the centuries and throughout the world there have been many beautiful and artistic forms of the cross.

ANCHOR

BUDDED

CALVARY

CELTIC

COPTIC

CROSSLET

EGYPTIAN

GREEK

JERUSALEM

JEWELED

LATIN

LORRAINE

MALTESE

PAPAL

PASSION

PATRIARCHAL

POTENT

RUSSIAN

SALTIRE

TAU

TRIUMPH

VOIDED

```
K  B  C  M  P  X  V  N  K  P  K  P  H  C
E  D  F  E  Y  A  I  O  J  A  E  A  P  O
E  U  E  Z  L  T  T  E  X  S  N  T  M  P
R  Z  F  D  A  T  R  E  U  S  I  R  U  T
G  O  O  L  I  U  I  Y  E  I  A  I  I  I
T  E  L  S  S  O  R  C  H  O  R  A  R  C
N  S  M  A  Y  A  V  R  K  N  R  R  T  H
V  A  L  A  V  Q  U  D  R  R  O  C  A  C
X  E  I  L  L  S  S  O  I  G  L  H  U  H
M  B  A  T  S  T  H  Y  P  A  P  A  L  L
R  C  K  I  P  C  E  J  E  W  E  L  E  D
M  H  A  Z  N  Y  V  S  B  U  D  D  E  D
H  N  X  A  I  X  G  D  E  J  E  W  Y  E
T  N  E  T  O  P  E  E  R  I  T  L  A  S
```

Answers on page 76

CROSSWORD FILL-IN NO. 1

DIRECTIONS
Answers for this puzzle are listed below. Across and Down words are mixed together. Find each word's correct position in the crossword grid. Some three-letter words are abbreviations.

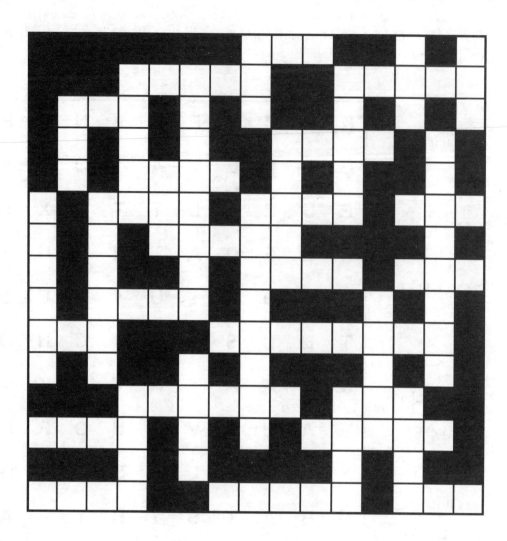

3 LETTERS	4 LETTERS	5 LETTERS	6 LETTERS	8 LETTERS
ALB	ACTS	AARON	ALTARS	BLESSING
ANN	AHAB	AGAPE	BARUCH	BROTHERS
ARK	ALMS	ALTAR	CHERUB	CIBORIUM
ASH	ARCH	AMBRY		CREATION
CCD	ARKS	AVILA		
CFX	BAAL	BANNS		
COL	BEAD	BIBLE		
COR	BODY	CREED		
CUP	CELL	DEVIL		
CYO	CITE			
DAN	CLAY			
DEN	COWL			

Answers on page 74

NUMBERS GAME NO. 1

How well do you know catechism numbers? Test your knowledge by answering the following questions.

1 To the number of gifts of the Holy Spirit, add the number of kinds of actual sin.   = _____

2 To the answer above, add the number of days from the resurrection to the ascension.   = _____

3 From the answer above, subtract the number of cardinal virtues.   = _____

4 From the answer above, subtract the number of marks of the Church times the number of theological virtues.   = _____

5 From the answer above, subtract the number of corporal works of mercy.   = _____

6 Divide the answer above by the number of natures Jesus possesses.   = _____

7 From the answer above, subtract the number of commandments.   = _____

Your final answer is the number of _____ in the Trinity.

Answers on page 93

BIBLICAL MENU

For which religious feast did God give the Israelites the following menu?

DINNER

Roasted Lamb (one-year-old male goat or sheep lamb)

Bitter Herbs

Unleavened Bread

Answers on page 93

PROPHETICAL & HISTORICAL BOOKS

The Old Testament is divided into several parts. Some of the books of the Old Testament are the books of the prophets and the historical books.

AMOS

BARUCH

CHRONICLES

DANIEL

ESTHER

EZEKIEL

EZRA

HABAKKUK

HAGGAI

HOSEA

ISAIAH

JEREMIAH

JOEL

JONAH

JUDITH

KINGS

LAMENTATIONS

MACCABEES

C	H	R	O	N	I	C	L	E	S	P	S	M	Z
K	U	K	K	A	B	A	H	W	O	N	U	E	E
H	H	A	N	O	J	S	E	D	O	H	P	H	C
B	A	Z	M	M	B	L	G	I	A	H	B	A	H
M	I	I	U	O	E	A	T	N	A	H	A	I	A
S	A	X	M	I	S	A	D	N	I	D	R	M	R
A	S	C	K	E	T	I	I	I	A	K	U	E	I
M	I	E	C	N	R	A	A	N	A	F	C	H	A
U	Z	K	E	A	H	E	I	G	L	H	H	E	H
E	T	M	E	O	B	E	J	Y	G	H	O	N	A
L	A	Z	S	D	L	E	M	A	L	A	C	H	I
L	R	E	H	T	S	E	E	Q	D	C	H	S	B
A	A	J	U	D	I	T	H	S	D	I	Y	H	D
T	O	B	I	T	L	E	O	J	L	M	U	X	F

MALACHI   NEHEMIAH   TOBIT

MICAH   OBADIAH   ZECHARIAH

NAHUM   SAMUEL   ZEPHANIAH

Answers on page 76

CALIFORNIA MISSIONS

El Camino Real is a well-known road in Californian history. It was along this way that the Spanish missionaries, following Spanish explorers, established the famous Spanish Mission System. These missions are prefixed by "San" or "Santa."

ANTONIO DE PADUA

BARBARA

BUENAVENTURA

CARLOS

CLARA

CRUZ

DIEGO

FERNANDO

FRANCISCO

GABRIEL

INES

JOSE

JUAN BAUTISTA

JUAN CAPISTRANO

LUIS OBISPO

LUIS REY

MIGUEL

RAFAEL

H	S	E	C	D	N	D	D	F	A	P	B	A	P	D
A	S	O	T	M	E	I	T	N	I	P	A	Z	Q	V
Q	N	F	Y	E	E	H	S	G	A	B	R	I	E	L
N	O	T	C	G	T	H	U	Y	U	T	B	Z	W	S
Z	E	S	O	J	K	G	M	Y	X	C	A	F	Z	X
Z	J	U	A	N	C	A	P	I	S	T	R	A	N	O
C	Y	A	T	S	I	T	U	A	B	N	A	U	J	P
J	A	Y	P	C	O	O	L	W	S	L	N	U	Z	S
L	M	R	F	A	M	D	D	N	Y	E	D	R	W	I
C	N	O	A	R	U	T	N	E	V	A	N	E	U	B
M	Q	Y	I	L	H	H	R	A	P	F	V	I	K	O
D	S	Z	W	O	C	S	I	C	N	A	R	F	G	S
E	N	X	H	S	I	T	W	X	L	R	D	C	X	I
R	R	L	E	U	G	I	M	E	R	P	E	U	G	U
Z	F	F	L	L	M	S	C	C	Y	L	T	F	A	L

Answers on page 76

CROSSWORD FILL-IN NO. 2

DIRECTIONS
Answers for this puzzle are listed below. Across and Down words are mixed together. Find each word's correct position in the crossword grid. Some three-letter words are abbreviations.

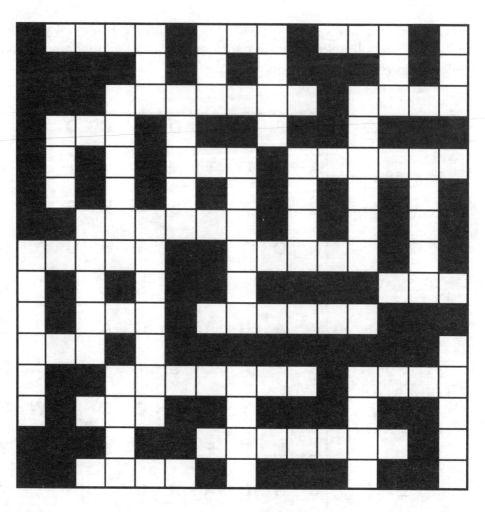

3 LETTERS	4 LETTERS	5 LETTERS	6 LETTERS	7 LETTERS
DEN	*ECCE*	EAGLE	EASTER	ETERNAL
EAR	EDOM	EPHOD	ERRORS	GABRIEL
EAT	*ELOI*	FAITH	FRIDAY	ITALIAN
ELI	EVIL	FIRST	FRUITS	JOACHIM
EPH	FREE	FROGS	GLORIA	
EZK	GOLD	JESUS	JOSIAH	
EZR	ICON		JOYFUL	
GAL	*IRAE*			
HRE	JEWS			
HVJ				
IHS				
JON				
JOS				

Answers on page 74

PORTRAITS

Each person on the right is associated with information on the left. Match each person with the appropriate information.

1	Leap of faith, city of Haran, patriarch	_____	Peter
2	"Open a window," chaplain, council	_____	John Paul II
3	Temple, wisdom, king	_____	Paul
4	John the Baptist, canticle, cousin	_____	Abraham
5	Theater, Mary, Polish	_____	Moses
6	Jesse, star, Goliath	_____	John XXIII
7	Soldier, Spanish, Society of Jesus	_____	David
8	Gentiles, preaching, epistles	_____	Solomon
9	Basket, burning bush, Exodus	_____	Elizabeth
10	Quick-tempered, keys, fisherman	_____	Ignatius Loyola

Answers on page 93

CRYPTOGRAM NO. 1

In this sentence, letters have been substituted for other letters. For example, "DJS DLAS JWM BQAS" is "THE TIME HAS COME." The words are in their correct order, with a space after each word. You can break the code by watching for the frequency of certain letters or the way letters are grouped. A single letter is usually "A" or "I." Groupings of two may be "it," "by," or "of," for example. This cryptogram is a common Bible phrase or catechism answer.

EBW CU JDS UMYNSTS ASCGE KDB TQWS

QVV JDCGEU QGW FSSYU JDST CG SOCUJSGZS.

Answers on page 93

CROSSWORD PUZZLE NO. 3

ACROSS

4   Very skilled person
8   He walked through the fiery furnace
11 "A time to seek, and a time to ____..." (Eccl 3:6)
13 Tell (slang)
14 Certain monks
15 "Ones," to Pierre
17 Copy
18 Nerd
19 Goddess of tillage
21 Monogram of the Holy Name of Jesus
22 Led the wise men
24 What Adam and Eve were forbidden to do regarding the fruit of a certain tree
27 Colors
29 Wind direction
31 Floor covering
33 Pertaining to the nonordained of the Church
35 Old Testament prophet or pop singer Billy
36 Biblical land
38 What the sky did when Jesus died
40 Peter's real name
42 Cat cry
43 Bric-a-____
45 ____ Gandolfo, summer residence of the pope
49 Certain Wednesday
50 Pop group
51 Blessing of throats occurs on his feast day
52 Cut

DOWN

1   Secretary of the prophet Jeremiah
2   _____ Pence
3   Explosive letters
4   Early Christians celebrated the ____ meal
5   Long cloak worn during Benediction
6   He parted the Red Sea
7   Annoying
9   Ruin
10 Period of history
11 "You are the ____ of the world" (Mt 5:14)
12 Holy woman, in Lyons (abbr.)
16 Brother of Abel
20 Paul, formerly
21 A divine name for Jesus found in the Gospel of John
23 Peruse
25 Hosea, in the Douay-Rheims version of the Bible
26 Muslim judge
28 Former name of Thailand
29 Jesus is the ___ of Man
30 Antiquity
31 Fits closely with
32 What Lazarus was already in when Jesus came to see him
34 Nativity scene
35 The Chosen People
37 Ethical
39 Hawaiian acacia
41 U.S. space agency
44 First of two Greek letters that are a monogram for Jesus
46 Number of the commandment that forbids us to covet our neighbor's goods
47 Jewish high priest and judge
48 Cut off

Answers on page 72

CAPTIVITY THROUGH POST-EXILIC PERIOD

The Exile is the story of the captivity of the Jews in Babylon.

AUGUSTUS CAESAR

BABYLONIAN CAPTIVITY

DIASPORA

EZRA

GREEK

HASMONEAN

HEROD ANTIPATER

INVASION

JERUSALEM

JUDAS MACCABEUS

KING CYRUS

MACCABEES

MATTATHIAS

NEHEMIAH

PERSIAN

PONTIUS PILATE

POST-EXILIC

PROPHET

QUIRINIUS

REBUILD

REMNANT

RESTORATION

ROMAN EMPIRE

SABBATH

SYNAGOGUE

TEMPLE TREASURY

TORAH

WALLS OF THE CITY

WISDOM BOOKS

ZACHARIAH

```
V I D N X S X P S U R Y C G N I K R B Y
W D N E A C A I O U F S G P I Q O A D R
F P Y V A I O B C N E G R B R A B D E U
K O S X A X S I B E T O S O J Y P N B S
Z Z H A W S T R B A P I M W L U E R R A
V A Y Z I U I A E H T A U O M C P E C E
X H C T I H C O E P N H N S F K T S I R
F S J H I C T T N E P I J A P A I T L T
S U E B A C C A M S A D U J P I X O I E
N I R M R R E P T N D F K I T E L R X L
E N U L Z T I H C T R P T Z U E S A E P
H I S Y E R T A T B A N Y G L W C T T M
E R A H E N P O H F A M O R C X A I S E
M I L S A T U Q P D O G K E E R G O O T
I U E N I R E E O H A S M O N E A N P Q
A Q M V R F O R U N V D L I U B E R Y V
H E I Q G B E T Y R A S B L R Z W O M X
R T M V O H G S Y G B R D I A S P O R A
Y A U G U S T U S C A E S A R W B B Q K
Z G M U S K O O B M O D S I W N X W A U
```

Answers on page 77

SAINTS OF THE MODERN ERA

Many saints have been named in the past two centuries.

BERNADETTE	CLARET	KIM	SAVIO
BIANCHI	CORDERO	KOLBE	SETON
CABRINI	COUDERC	LWANGA	STEIN
CHANEL	DON BOSCO	NEUMANN	VIANNEY
CHONG	GIANELLI	PALLOTTI	

```
C G N O H C E N R E T C P C
T H R Q N Z N W T P B L A R
C G A O I A N T C I P J L E
O Y T N M S E E A K M M L D
M E F U E D O N B O S C O U
S G E O A L C X L L R Q T O
X N I N R H S W T A O E T C
W T R A I E A C A J C K I H
O E O Q N N D U O J L N R R
B W I V G E N R A I A D T E
P F V A A X L A O H R X I U
V I A N N E Y L K C E G R N
E L S T E I N G I I T H K O
I N I R B A C W C O M Q E L
```

Answers on page 78

CROSSWORD PUZZLE NO. 4

ACROSS

2 It's sometimes not enough
6 Ancestor of Jesus
10 Gov't lawyer
12 Fall short
13 Catholic spirituality program
15 Enemy of Israel
17 Digit
19 Saint ___ de Beaupré
20 Land east of Eden
21 German masculine determiner
22 Old Testament book (abbr.)
23 What Abraham was
26 Fifth book of the Bible
28 Monogram of the Holy Name of Jesus
30 Country to the northeast of Israel
31 They have a ball
33 Sibilate
34 Religious ed. classes
35 "To be," in Latin
38 First king of Israel
40 Irritate
41 Mother of Jesus (abbr.)
43 Member of a rel. order
44 Tribe of Israel
45 Preposition
47 First commandment opening
49 Penpoint
51 Play part
53 A vestment
54 Certain volcano
55 Fixes socks
57 Christian and pre-Christian
59 ALF
60 Encounter
61 Cell (comb.)

DOWN

1 Adam and Eve were cast out of here
2 Franciscans (abbr.)
3 Old Testament book (abbr.)
4 Referred to a biblical passage
5 "... _____, lema sabachthani?" (Mk 15:34)
6 Either's partner
7 Endure
8 Boredom
9 Where Daniel was
11 "Lord," in Hebrew
14 "___ give you thanks for your great glory."
16 Aromas
18 Finished
24 Liturgy
25 "I AM WHO _____" (Ex 3:14)
27 Old Testament history book
29 Envision
31 CCC + CCCL
32 Son of Adam
33 Prophetic book of the Bible (abbr.)
34 Offices through which the pope administers the affairs of the Church
36 Perfume
37 Lourdes or Fatima
39 "___ it was in the beginning…"
40 Form of "to be"
42 Bishop's hat
44 Box containing holy oils
46 Novena number
48 Catholic actor, ____ Guinness
50 Restrain
51 In the year of the Lord, in Latin (abbr.)
52 Shaft on a car
54 Wind direction
56 Holy person (abbr.)
58 Near to

Answers on page 72

SAINTS & EMBLEMS

Can you match the symbolic object or sign usually associated, according to tradition, with these saints?

1	Agnes	_____	Two ravens
2	Patrick	_____	Ox
3	Blaise	_____	Lamb
4	Cecilia	_____	Taper
5	Dominic	_____	Organ
6	Helena	_____	Rosary
7	Peter	_____	Winged man
8	Jerome	_____	Sword
9	Luke	_____	Tears
10	Matthew	_____	Cross
11	Meinrad	_____	Keys
12	Michael	_____	Arrows
13	Monica	_____	Children
14	Vincent de Paul	_____	Shamrock
15	Sebastian	_____	Lion

Answers on page 94

THE PASSION

The paschal mystery is the suffering, death, and resurrection of the Lord. Paschal refers to the fact that these events occurred during Passover (Pesch).

AGONY IN THE GARDEN

ANNAS

APOSTLES

ARREST

BETRAYAL

BLOOD AND WATER

BURIAL

CAIAPHAS

CLOAK

CROWN OF THORNS

CRUCIFIXION

FALL THREE TIMES

FRIDAY

GETHSEMANE

GOLGOTHA

HEROD

A	G	N	Z	T	E	E	F	F	O	G	N	I	H	S	A	W	S
P	N	O	I	T	C	E	R	R	U	S	E	R	C	P	T	D	T
O	I	I	P	F	H	R	N	P	B	X	D	E	K	A	O	L	C
S	P	X	O	S	E	M	I	T	E	E	R	H	T	L	L	A	F
T	P	I	N	S	R	E	R	N	T	Y	A	D	I	R	F	I	A
L	I	F	T	O	O	N	D	N	R	A	G	E	B	Y	C	N	V
E	H	I	I	R	D	A	E	A	A	R	E	C	L	R	Y	E	T
S	W	C	U	C	U	M	H	I	Y	V	H	W	O	W	A	D	R
H	S	U	S	E	V	E	N	L	A	S	T	W	O	R	D	S	E
I	A	R	P	H	B	S	A	S	L	R	N	T	D	G	N	R	P
G	H	C	I	T	U	H	S	Q	I	O	I	S	A	O	U	E	P
H	P	E	L	F	R	T	K	A	F	T	Y	E	N	L	S	T	U
P	A	Y	A	O	I	E	L	T	M	O	N	R	D	G	A	E	S
R	I	M	T	Y	A	G	H	N	A	M	O	R	W	O	N	P	T
I	A	Y	E	A	L	O	X	B	T	B	G	A	A	T	N	O	S
E	C	E	I	W	R	E	V	O	S	S	A	P	T	H	A	A	A
S	I	M	O	N	O	F	C	Y	R	E	N	E	E	A	V	L	L
T	M	V	S	J	U	D	A	S	I	S	C	A	R	I	O	T	Y

HIGH PRIEST

JUDAS ISCARIOT

LAST SUPPER

NAILS

PASSOVER

PETER'S DENIAL

PONTIUS PILATE

RESURRECTION

ROMAN

SANHEDRIN

SEVEN LAST WORDS

SIMON OF CYRENE

SUNDAY

TOMB

TRIAL

WASHING OF FEET

WAY OF THE CROSS

WHIPPING

Answers on page 78

I CAN NAME THAT ANSWER IN SEVEN CLUES!

Seven is a significant theological number. On the seventh day God rested; the Ark of the Covenant was carried around Jericho seven times before the walls came down; there are seven miracles in John's Gospel. See if you can identify the following persons, places, or things in seven clues or less. Give yourself one point for each clue you needed to complete the puzzle. If you could not answer a category at all, give yourself eight points for that category. You are aiming for a LOW score. A score of 15 or less is outstanding. A score of 20 is very good. A score of 28 is good. Good luck.

I PERSON

1   Lived in the thirteenth century   _____

2   Born in Italy   _____

3   Composed the *Panis Angelicus*   _____

4   Taught at the University of Paris   _____

5   Dominican   _____

6   Called the "Dumb Ox"   _____

7   Wrote the *Summa Theologica*   _____

II STRUCTURE

1   Designed by Bernini   _____

2   Building completed in 1626   _____

3   Basilica for the patriarch of Constantinople   _____

4   In Italy   _____

5   Second largest Catholic church building   _____

6   One of the seven main churches in Rome   _____

7   Contains the Sistine Chapel   _____

Answers on page 94

III PROCESS

1 Infallible declaration _____

2 Christian virtue _____

3 Martyrs _____

4 Dulia _____

5 Veneration _____

6 Miracles _____

7 Step after beatification _____

IV APPARITION

1 1531 _____

2 Tepeyac _____

3 Mantle _____

4 Build a church _____

5 Roses _____

6 Juan Diego _____

7 Mexico _____

Answers on page 94

CATHOLIC TERMS

Find the words in this list of popular Catholic devotional items, practices, and significant terms.

ADORATION   CHARACTER   CRUCIFIX   GOOD WORKS

BENEDICTION   CHARISM   DEVOTIONS   GRACE

CANONIZATION   CONSECRATION   FAITH   HOLY HOUR

CATECHUMEN   CONTRITION   GAUDETE   INDULGENCE

LITANY

MARIAN

MINISTRY

MONK

MYSTERIES

PROCESSION

PSALTER

PURGATORY

ROGATION

ROSARY

SCAPULAR

SOLEMNITY

STATIONS

TRADITION

TRIDUUM

```
F T P M A R I A N Q R S G W P F T
A R U S E Y Q J B S L Y N R E P W
Q A A I N R A L U P A C S L A N P
C D S R E T C A R A H C E L S C S
A I X A M S E W S N O I T A T S E
N T K H U I E E C N E G L U D N I
O I J C H N H H S H O L Y H O U R
N O I T C I D E N E B I R Y I A E
I N M Y E M C I O X R B T R D S T
Z C O N T R I T I O N O T O B O S
A Q N A A X U F S D O G R T V L Y
T F K T C E I A S N I A I A F E M
I Q I I X C R X E C T U D G A M D
O O U L U Y Y I C I A D U R I N K
N S K R O W D O O G G E U U T I I
J D C A R X W N R U O T M P H T R
D U R E T L A S P L R E M P Y Y O
```

Answers on page 78

CARDINALS OF THE U.S. (1875–PRESENT)

Cardinal is an honorary title given to a bishop. The cardinals select the pope from among their group.

BAUM

BERNARDIN

BEVILACQUA

BRENNAN

CARBERRY

CODY

COOKE

CUSHING

DEARDEN

DOUGHERTY

FARLEY

GIBBONS

GLENNON

HAYES

HICKEY

KEELER

KROL

LAW

J	V	Y	E	L	R	A	F	W	O	Y	G	M	U	D
H	S	T	R	I	T	C	H	C	L	N	U	P	G	K
A	H	R	E	Y	E	M	O	A	I	A	Z	E	N	R
Y	E	E	M	X	L	N	S	N	B	M	W	R	I	O
E	H	H	Y	G	N	O	N	N	E	L	G	Y	H	L
S	A	G	R	O	R	A	A	Y	B	L	L	T	S	A
N	N	U	R	I	M	N	I	E	L	E	D	N	U	M
A	I	O	E	E	N	P	V	K	O	P	F	I	C	O
P	X	D	B	E	L	I	I	C	E	S	E	C	M	B
W	E	M	R	B	L	E	O	I	O	K	L	M	U	O
M	R	B	A	A	I	N	E	H	M	O	O	N	E	Y
A	O	I	C	H	N	G	A	K	S	C	D	O	N	L
I	T	Q	G	E	O	R	A	K	O	Z	S	T	C	E
D	U	K	L	H	A	N	E	D	R	A	E	D	H	W
A	A	L	U	Y	T	Y	Y	B	R	I	T	T	E	R

MAHONY	MEDEIROS	O'BOYLE	SHEHAN
MAIDA	MEYER	O'CONNELL	SPELLMAN
MANNING	MOONEY	O'CONNOR	STRITCH
MCCLOSKEY	MUENCH	O'HARA	SZOKA
MCINTYRE	MUNDELEIN	RITTER	WRIGHT

Answers on page 78

ACROSTIC

Using the clues on the left, solve the following puzzles. Each letter in the answer is assigned a number. Using those numbers, fill in the blanks at the bottom to reveal the name of an important Catholic site in the United States.

CLUES   **ANSWER**

A   Joseph was given a many-colored one

___ ___ ___ ___
27   8   30   1

B   Three Persons in one God

___ ___ ___ ___ ___ ___
20 14 40 28   9   3

C   Belief

___ ___ ___ ___ ___
19   5 23 39   2

D   Office time

___ ___ ___ ___ ___ ___
24 26   6 15 35 12

E   Room off the main part of a church

___ ___ ___ ___ ___ ___
33 21 10 38 17 29

F   Start of darkness on the day of Jesus' death

___ ___ ___ ___
4   18 34 16

G   "Heaven," in Paris

___ ___ ___ ___
36   7 32 11

H   What Jesus called Nazareth

___ ___ ___ ___
13 41 25 37

I   Tool of trade for Peter and Andrew

___ ___ ___
42 22 31

___ ___ ___ ___ ___ ___ ___ ___ ___ ___ ___ ___ ___ ___ ___ ___ ___
 1   2   3   4   5   6   7   8   9 10 11 12 13 14 15 16 17

___ ___ ___ ___ ___ ___ ___ ___ ___ ___ ___ ___ ___ ___ ___
18 19 20 21 22 23 24 25 26 27 28 29 30 31 32

___ ___ ___ ___ ___ ___ ___ ___ ___ ___
33 34 35 36 37 38 39 40 41 42

Answers on page 94

ENCYCLICAL MATCH

When you were in school you probably learned the names of some important encyclicals. Below is a mixed-up list of the names of modern-day encyclicals. See if you can re-match the words and put the list together correctly. Give yourself extra credit if you can match the date to the correct encyclical.

	ENCYCLICAL	DATE	
1	*Humanae Hominis*	1891	_____
2	*Mater et Spiritu*	1943	_____
3	*Ecclesiam Progressio*	1947	_____
4	*Rerum Novarum*	1961	_____
5	*Mysterium in Terris*	1963	_____
6	*Populorum Vitae*	1964	_____
7	*Redemptor Dei*	1965	_____
8	*Mediator Fidei*	1967	_____
9	*Divino Afflante Suam*	1968	_____
10	*Pacem Magistra*	1979	_____

Answers on page 94

WORD BUILDER NO. 2

RESURRECTION

Form all the four- and five-letter words you can by using only the letters in the word **RESURRECTION**. You may use a letter more than once in a word only if it appears more than once in **RESURRECTION**. Words beginning with capital letters, plurals, contractions, and hyphenated, slang, poetic, and foreign words are not allowed. Check our list of four- and five-letter words.

Answers on page 94

CELESTIAL BEINGS

Angels and heavenly beings have been a traditional belief in the Church since its beginning. An angel spoke to Mary about becoming the mother of Jesus, and angels announced the birth of Christ to the shepherds.

ANGEL	CHERUBIM	GABRIEL	JOPHIEL
ARCHANGEL	COUNSELOR	GOVERNOR	JOPHKIEL
CHAMAEL	DOMINATIONS	HERALD	MESSENGER
			MICHAEL
			MINISTER
			POWERS
			PRESENCE
			PRINCIPALITIES
			RAPHAEL
			SERAPHIM
			THRONES
			URIEL
			VIRTUES
			ZADKIEL

```
S  R  C  C  E  P  Q  J  Y  L  X  M  M  L  S
C  N  N  H  O  C  O  U  E  B  Y  I  I  E  E
J  O  O  W  E  P  N  A  F  R  G  C  H  G  U
P  O  E  I  H  R  M  E  O  H  O  H  P  N  T
H  R  P  K  T  A  U  L  S  W  V  A  A  A  R
S  E  I  H  H  A  E  B  S  E  E  E  R  H  I
O  E  R  C  I  S  N  L  I  E  R  L  E  C  V
L  X  I  A  N  E  V  I  E  M  N  P  S  R  N
R  O  E  U  L  T  L  J  M  I  O  O  M  A  H
X  P  O  Y  U  D  A  X  L  O  R  I  R  V  N
R  C  R  E  T  S  I  N  I  M  D  U  S  H  S
M  E  S  S  E  N  G  E  R  L  E  G  N  A  T
S  E  I  T  I  L  A  P  I  C  N  I  R  P  X
L  E  A  H  P  A  R  G  A  B  R  I  E  L  O
F  R  Z  A  D  K  I  E  L  S  K  F  M  C  C
```

Answers on page 79

CATHOLIC MEDALS

```
E U H I Z E D Y Y G K X V P P M
A M X J Q T X N C B E F P Y R A
N Q M R B O R B P B V Y F O P R
X P U A E N I M R A L L E B X I
S T V I N C E N T D E P A U L A
C A I R N U U A C L S P G Q S N
A K T G D A E M L I X A U I R L
R P J I F B S L G E U U N B O I
I M S S L B S N D D D G O P L B
T F Z V X E U C I A I N C F L R
A A S G C M D U D S L Q E S E A
S N I P F U M I N V O Z X M R R
I I B I N X T I F Q L J O Y E Y
S G D P A T R O N A L J M N V F
H E R A T E A L V Z N F U C O E
I R L A C N N H T G M I J N P Q
```

Answers on page 79

AQUINAS	GAUDIUM	PATRONAL
BELLARMINE	INSIGNIS	POVERELLO
CARITAS	LAETARE	REGINA
EMMANUEL D'ALZON	MARIAN LIBRARY	SIGNUM FIDEI
FIDELITAS	MENDEL	ST. VINCENT DE PAUL

TRADITIONAL VESTMENTS & INSIGNIA

The clergy of the Catholic Church wear (and have worn) certain distinctive pieces of clothing or adornment. Much of the clothing dates back to the Roman period when it was simply traditional dress for the time.

ALB
AMICE
BIRETTA
BUSKINS
CAPPA MAGNA
CASSOCK
CHASUBLE
CINCTURE
COPE
CROSIER
DALMATIC
FALDA
GLOVES
MANIPLE
MANTELLETTA
MITER
MORSE
MOZZETTA
PECTORAL CROSS
RING
ROCHET
SANDALS
SKULLCAP
STAFF
STOLE
SUBCINCTORIUM
SURPLICE
TIARA
TUNICLE

```
P  B  I  F  F  A  T  S  L  A  D  N  A  S
O  E  L  P  I  N  A  M  T  B  C  C  B  N
Q  L  C  A  P  P  A  M  A  G  N  A  C  I
I  B  S  T  O  L  E  A  M  C  X  P  W  K
M  U  I  R  O  T  C  N  I  C  B  U  S  S
F  S  B  Y  E  R  U  T  C  N  I  C  K  U
M  A  K  I  O  C  A  E  E  L  V  G  U  B
I  H  L  S  R  M  I  L  D  Y  S  L  L  T
T  C  I  D  L  E  T  L  C  O  J  O  L  U
E  E  F  A  A  E  T  E  P  R  Q  V  C  N
R  P  D  A  R  A  I  T  H  R  O  E  A  I
I  M  O  Z  Z  E  T  T  A  C  U  S  P  C
N  F  K  C  O  S  S  A  C  Q  O  S  S  L
G  K  P  L  U  M  A  O  J  M  O  R  S  E
```

Answers on page 79

DISTINCTIVE POPES

Popes have been among the most influential figures of the Western world. See if you can identify these first, last, and only popes.

1   First pope to voluntarily resign   _____

2   Last pope to resign   _____

3   First pope to change his name   _____

4   Last pope to keep his own name   _____

5   Only English pope   _____

6   Only Polish pope   _____

7   First pope to address the United Nations   _____

8   Last pope to be canonized   _____

9   Last anti-pope   _____

10   First twentieth-century pope to be canonized   _____

Select from this list:

Adrian IV	John Paul II
Celestine V	Leo XIII
Felix V	Marcellus II
Gregory XII	Paul VI
John II	Pius X

Answers on page 94

CROSSWORD FILL-IN NO. 3

DIRECTIONS

Answers for this puzzle are listed below. Across and Down words are mixed together. Find each word's correct position in the crossword grid. Some words are abbreviations.

3 LETTERS
- JOB
- JON
- LAW
- LEO
- LOT
- MAY
- MRE
- NUN
- OFM
- OIL
- *ORA*

4 LETTERS
- JEWS
- LAIC
- LEAH
- LENT
- LEVI
- LORD
- LOVE
- LUST
- MEAL
- MEEK
- MSGR
- NOEL
- OSEE
- PAUL

5 LETTERS
- MARKS
- MICAH
- NAHUM
- NINTH

6 LETTERS
- JOYFUL
- LETTER
- MANGER
- MARTHA
- MARTYR
- NOVENA

8 LETTERS
- ORDAINED
- PARABLES

Answers on page 74

INFANCY STORIES

The Infancy Narratives are the stories of the birth of Jesus. They are found only in the Gospels of Matthew and Luke.

ANGEL

ANNA

ANNUNCIATION

BETHLEHEM

CENSUS

CIRCUMCISION

DIVORCE

DREAM

EGYPT

ELIZABETH

EMMANUEL

GALILEE

GENEALOGY

HEROD

JOHN
THE BAPTIST

JOSEPH

S	K	T	M	S	M	W	N	R	M	B	I	H	T	A	H	E	T
H	E	A	A	A	H	A	E	E	A	Y	K	S	O	N	G	E	P
T	R	H	E	C	Z	E	H	H	N	T	I	D	C	N	I	L	L
Y	W	R	T	A	I	E	P	E	T	T	S	I	V	U	H	I	U
M	D	O	R	O	L	F	M	H	P	T	R	N	J	N	T	L	K
F	A	E	T	H	L	E	I	A	E	C	A	D	O	C	S	A	E
S	T	N	T	U	S	C	B	N	U	R	S	M	S	I	O	G	P
H	U	E	G	I	R	E	G	M	G	I	D	C	E	A	M	H	Z
L	B	S	W	E	H	T	C	N	M	A	M	S	P	T	E	T	Z
E	B	Z	N	T	R	I	L	E	I	H	M	Z	H	I	H	E	Z
G	G	D	N	E	S	J	O	E	E	L	E	S	X	O	T	B	E
N	Q	H	T	I	C	N	A	E	D	W	D	R	O	N	F	A	C
A	O	N	O	T	I	R	I	P	S	O	E	D	O	K	O	Z	H
J	M	N	E	G	Y	P	T	H	N	V	V	Z	A	D	N	I	A
N	O	I	T	A	T	N	E	S	E	R	P	E	V	W	O	L	R
G	E	N	E	A	L	O	G	Y	A	N	N	A	S	B	S	E	I
N	O	R	O	O	M	I	N	T	H	E	I	N	N	Z	M	P	A
L	E	U	N	A	M	M	E	D	I	V	O	R	C	E	A	L	H

LUKE	NO ROOM IN THE INN	STAR
MAGNIFICAT	PRESENTATION	SWADDLING CLOTHES
MANGER	SHEPHERDS	TWO TURTLEDOVES
MARY	SIMEON	WISE MEN
MATTHEW	SON OF THE MOST HIGH	ZECHARIAH
NAZARETH	SPIRIT	

Answers on page 80

JUMBLED WORDS NO. 1

Unscramble these jumbles, then arrange the circled letters to form the answer to the question below.

AERUTC □ ○ □ □ □ ○

SELRAI □ ○ ○ □ □ □

DLSESBE □ □ □ ○ □ □ ○

PTSIABM □ ○ □ ○ □ □ □

TRUYIGL □ □ □ □ □ ○ ○

PLTAOSE □ □ ○ ○ □ □ □

What "holy" day is celebrated in England on August 12?

ANSWER __ __   __ __ __ __ __ __ '__   __ __ __

Answers on page 94

JUMBLED WORDS NO. 2

HRTOSPEP ○ □ ○ □ □ □ □ □

SHIMCAR ○ □ ○ □ □ □

EKELNRE ○ □ □ □ □ ○ □

TIRENEYT □ ○ ○ □ □ □ □ □

CURATISHE □ □ ○ ○ □ □ □ □ □

What bird, often pictured on tombs, is a symbol of resurrection?

ANSWER __ __ __   __ __ __ __ __ __

Answers on page 94

HOLY DAYS OF OBLIGATION

In addition to Sundays, holy days of obligation are days when Catholics are required to go to Mass and refrain from unnecessary work in order to dedicate the day to God. The dates for the holy days in the United States are listed below. See if you can fill in the name of the holy day.

1   January 1   _____

2   40 days after Easter   _____

3   August 15   _____

4   November 1   _____

5   December 8   _____

6   December 25   _____

Answers on page 94

THE CHRISTMAS QUIZ

The story of Jesus' birth is told only in the Gospels of Matthew and Luke. How well do you know the story of Jesus' birth? Read each statement below. Which events are recorded in Matthew and which events in Luke?

		MATTHEW	LUKE
1	The wise men visit the Holy Family	_____	_____
2	Joseph and Mary travel to Bethlehem for a census	_____	_____
3	Jesus is laid in a manger	_____	_____
4	Herod orders the killing of baby boys	_____	_____
5	There is no room in the inn	_____	_____
6	In a dream Joseph is told to marry Mary	_____	_____

Answers on page 94

RELIGIOUS ORDERS

Religious orders provide valuable services of various kinds to the community and participate in the mission of proclaiming the gospel.

BENEDICTINE

CARMELITE

CHARITY

CHRISTIAN BROTHER

CISTERCIAN

CLARETIAN

DIVINE PROVIDENCE

FRIARS MINOR

GOOD SHEPHERD

GREY NUNS

HOLY CROSS

IMMACULATE HEART OF MARY

JOSEPHITE

LITTLE SISTERS OF THE POOR

LORETTO

MARIST

MARYKNOLL

MERCY

OBLATE

ORATORIAN

ORDER OF PREACHERS

PASSIONIST

PAULIST

PRECIOUS BLOOD

SALESIAN

SOCIETY OF JESUS

URSULINE

VISITATION

XAVIERIAN

```
J O S E P H I T E E Y C H A R I T Y O L L M
F R I A R S M I N O R U K F M S M F R I G A
E T A L B O A I C V A Y O W O R N E D T Z R
T Q G Y U F L C I Y M U S C E N N K E T M Y
E W Z V Y U D S I V F S I H U I Z I R L I K
J L B F S Q I U M S O E T N T L E Q O E P N
V K E R L T J A H R T O Y C E P S D F S A O
A Z U U A Q R X C Y R E I C S P G R P I S L
C J L T H I Q Y O B A D R X R G V E R S S L
O O I O S A L F N O E J O C D E V H E T I N
Q O C T R O J A R N H U N Y I D M P A E O A
N C O D H E I A E X E Y S Z N A Y E C R N I
I E S H S T T B R F T Y C D A L N H H S I T
P H L U S O B T S I A R V S I D C S E O S E
E B S I R D C M O N L K P P S Q L D R F T R
J W R I D O O L B S U O I C E R P O S T P A
G H A O K X Z D P V C N X G L V V O H H A L
C N A I R E I V A X A M Y I A X L G D E U C
H J Z P R I J Z D H M L Z E S Q K N C P L V
N K X X V E T I L E M R A C R D X S Q O I M
B B G V J H M Q W E I V S N X G P W C O S L
D I V I N E P R O V I D E N C E P A B R T E
```

Answers on page 81

SAINTS

The saints are those who have died and are venerated for their virtuous lives.

BEATIFY

BLESSED

CANONIZE

COMMUNION

CULT

DEVOTION

DULIA

FEAST DAY

GLORY

HEAVEN

HERO

HOLY

INSPIRATION

INTERCESSORS

LITANY

MARTYR

MIRACLE

NOVENA

PATRON

RELIGIOUS

ROLE MODEL

VENERATION

```
L N P E J V U N Y X I V M A Z Y
D F O U L Q V N O N N A M I L L
S E A I L C A U S V T K S O E P
O A V I N T A P Q B E P H D G A
H S A O I U I R E B R N O G F T
I T S L T R M A I D C M A D L R
O D U U A I T M U M E G S I C O
X A O T M I O L O L S C Z Z E N
H Y I S F C I N O C S Y R O L G
E O G Y S A L R D T O I W G L O
N O I T A R E N E V R N T G G R
Z S L M A R T Y R Z S E O L S E
S Z E C A N O N I Z E V B C U H
G K R U D E S S E L B A E J C C
S L S Z V F K I R F E E V X P S
H M B D F R B V B M T H R E O P
```

Answers on page 84

NEW TESTAMENT BOOKS

See if you can fill in the missing letters for the books of the New Testament below. All missing letters are consonants.

1 __ A __ E __

2 __ O __ A __ __

3 __ __ I __ I __ __ I A __ __

4 __ A __ __ __ E __

5 __ E __ O __ __ __ __ E __ __ A __ O __ I A __ __

6 __ __ I __ E __ O __

7 __ E __ O __ __ __ E __ E __

8 __ A __ __

9 __ I __ U __

10 __ U __ E

11 __ E __ E __ A __ I O __

12 __ I __ __ __ __ E __ E __

13 __ U __ E

14 __ I __ __ __ __ O __ I __ __ __ I A __ __

15 __ O __ O __ __ I A __ __

16 __ I __ __ __ __ O __ __

17 __ A __ A __ I A __ __

18 __ O __ __

19 __ __ I __ __ __ O __ __

20 __ E __ __ E __ __

21 __ E __ O __ __ __ I __ O __ __ __

22 E __ __ E __ I A __ __

23 __ I __ __ __ __ __ E __ __ A __ O __ I A __ __

24 __ E __ O __ __ __ O __ __

25 __ I __ __ __ __ I __ O __ __ __

Answers on page 95

PATRON SAINTS

Patron saints are an ancient tradition in the Catholic Church. A patron saint is a saint who is venerated as a special intercessor before God. See if you can match the saint and the cause/activity of which he or she is a patron.

1	Luke	_____	Accountants
2	Vincent de Paul	_____	Orators
3	Francis of Assisi	_____	Priests
4	John of God	_____	Ecologists
5	Francis Xavier	_____	Catholic schools
6	John Vianney	_____	Charitable societies
7	Thomas Aquinas	_____	Artists
8	Matthew	_____	Foreign missions
9	John Chrysostom	_____	Hospitals
10	Aloysius Gonzaga	_____	Youth

Answers on page 95

CRYPTOGRAM NO. 2

In this sentence letters have been substituted for other letters. For example, "DJS DLAS JWM BQAS" is "THE TIME HAS COME." The words are in their correct order, with a space after each word. You can break the code by watching for the frequency of certain letters or the way letters are grouped. A single letter is usually "A" or "I." Groupings of two may be "it," "by," or "of," for example. This cryptogram is a common Bible phrase or catechism answer.

P WPLEPGMVQ   NW PV FSQAPEK WNJV

NVWQNQSQMK OB LUENWQ QF JNZM JEPLM.

Answers on page 95

ENCOUNTERING GOD

Sacraments are encounters with God. In the Catholic tradition, there are seven sacraments that are regarded as instituted by Christ.

ABSOLUTION

ANOINTING

BAPTISM

BREAD

CHARACTER

CONFESSION

CONFIRMATION

EFFICACIOUS

ENCOUNTER WITH GOD

EUCHARIST

FORGIVENESS

FORM

GIVES GRACE

HEALING

HOLY ORDERS

INDELIBLE

INITIATION

INSTITUTED BY CHRIST

LAYING ON OF HANDS

MARRIAGE

OIL

OUTWARD SIGN

PRIMARY SYMBOL

PROMISE

RECONCILIATION

SACRAMENT OF THE SICK

SEVEN

SIGN OF THE CROSS

VIATICUM

VOCATION

VOW

WATER

WINE

```
W S I G N O F T H E C R O S S E O S N N
I E N N C P Y T N E B F N S F I A Z O O
N L S D G Z R E S A S O O F L C C G I I
E B T A X I V I P I I I R R C O P T T
I I I E S E S T M S R C M A M A N V A U
N L T R S D I D S A A A M O N Y F O I L
I E U B Q S N E R C R E H O R E I C L O
T D T S M H F A I A N Y I C G P R A I S
I N E S T N O O H T W N S A U U M T C B
A I D V O C U L O F T T I Y Y E A I N A
T O B C P S Q F Y I O R U B M N T O O H
I F Y R V D T Q N O R N R O X B I N C R
O X C Q G H G G L A R I O N V B O T E T
N X H S E F C W M X S D Q G L Y N L R Q
H O R S D O G H T I W R E T N U O C N E
R G I V E S G R A C E O I R F I P L X W
W C S S E N E V I G R O F D S T Y Y W S
K N T V I A T I C U M R E T C A R A H C
G N I L A E H W A T E R W O V M X Q L V
J B W A J P C Z S F P B A T X R C I C O
```

Answers on page 82

EPISTLES

Epistles are letters. Paul wrote many letters to the churches he founded. Other apostles also wrote letters to the Church in general.

CATHOLIC

COLOSSIANS

CORINTHIANS

DIVERSITY
OF GIFTS

DOERS OF
THE WORD

DOXOLOGY

EPHESIANS

FAITH, HOPE,
AND LOVE

GALATIANS

GREETING

HEBREWS

JAMES

JOHN

JUDE

JUSTIFICATION
BY FAITH

LETTER

H	C	W	G	E	W	E	L	O	Y	B	T	O	C	L	T	W	S	D	R	N	T
G	T	K	A	J	P	C	P	W	A	I	N	A	Z	H	P	T	V	O	E	O	J
T	K	I	L	S	K	R	D	H	M	E	T	H	E	Q	R	B	C	E	T	M	A
K	D	X	A	O	N	U	I	O	E	H	Z	S	K	A	D	J	W	R	E	E	L
E	Q	U	T	F	M	A	T	G	O	S	S	Y	P	D	F	S	Y	S	P	L	G
S	Z	A	I	R	Y	H	I	L	H	A	I	Y	G	O	L	O	X	O	D	I	A
S	H	Y	A	E	Y	B	I	H	L	T	N	A	H	Z	R	I	O	F	D	H	S
P	V	Q	N	V	R	C	N	O	T	A	U	J	N	Q	O	S	A	T	U	P	N
Y	H	E	S	O	M	E	N	O	M	N	S	S	K	S	N	H	C	H	D	M	A
K	A	O	W	L	M	I	T	Y	I	E	I	M	E	A	U	W	R	E	M	E	I
Q	P	E	Z	D	A	X	D	T	M	T	E	R	I	O	M	W	U	W	D	G	P
C	Y	K	I	N	N	O	C	A	E	C	A	S	O	F	F	D	L	O	N	V	P
W	T	M	S	A	B	N	J	H	J	L	S	C	Z	C	E	W	C	R	S	W	I
H	D	I	V	E	R	S	I	T	Y	O	F	G	I	F	T	S	E	D	A	J	L
E	V	J	N	P	B	D	G	I	L	I	T	P	H	F	M	E	S	A	Y	S	I
B	G	O	O	O	A	N	O	O	R	G	R	E	E	T	I	N	G	D	L	R	H
R	J	R	I	H	I	U	C	T	N	E	M	A	T	S	E	T	W	E	N	T	P
E	U	K	K	H	N	E	L	E	S	N	A	M	O	R	A	A	S	X	E	Q	H
W	D	U	C	T	D	G	P	I	O	B	D	B	C	C	I	W	U	U	Y	F	D
S	E	A	K	I	F	P	V	B	N	C	I	Q	V	M	I	D	Z	G	J	U	E
B	E	N	M	A	N	W	V	S	T	E	T	I	T	U	S	U	T	C	H	J	M
T	T	B	E	F	D	W	U	T	W	E	N	T	Y	O	N	E	W	P	I	F	L

NEW
TESTAMENT

ONE BODY,
MANY PARTS

PAULINE

PETER

PHILEMON

PHILIPPIANS

RIGHT USE
OF WEALTH

ROMANS

TEACHING

THESSALONIANS

TIMOTHY

TITUS

TWENTY-ONE

Answers on page 83

NUMBERS GAME NO. 2

How well do you know biblical numbers? Test your knowledge by answering the following questions.

1   Add the number of apostles to the number of miracles in John.   = _____

2   To the answer above, add the number of days it rained in Genesis.   = _____

3   From the answer to the above, subtract the number of times Peter denied Jesus.   = _____

4   To the answer above, add the number of days of Creation (including the day God rested) times two.   = _____

5   From the answer to the above, subtract the accepted age of Jesus when he began preaching.   = _____

What is your final answer? Read Exodus 34:27–28. How does this relate to your answer?

Answers on page 95

CRYPTOGRAM NO. 3

In this sentence letters have been substituted for other letters. For example, "DJS DLAS JWM BQAS" is "THE TIME HAS COME." The words are in their correct order, with a space after each word. You can break the code by watching for the frequency of certain letters or the way letters are grouped. A single letter is usually "A" or "I." Groupings of two may be "it," "by," or "of," for example. This cryptogram is a common Bible phrase or catechism answer.

XJC   XJCUPUKHBMP   SHDXECR   MDC   LMHXJ

JUYC   MOV   BJMDHXA.

Answers on page 95

LITURGICAL OBJECTS

See if you can match the liturgical object to its definition.

1	Tall wine vessel for Mass	____	Ciborium
2	Instrument for sprinkling holy water	____	Chalice
3	Container for hosts distributed in Communion	____	Monstrance
4	Annual calendar of directions for each day's Mass	____	Corporal
5	Wine and water containers	____	Ordo
6	Square of linen cloth placed upon the altar	____	Pyx
7	Container for carrying the Communion host outside of church	____	Cruets
8	Container for exposition of the Blessed Sacrament	____	Aspergillum
9	Vessel for burning incense	____	Censer
10	Cup that holds the wine	____	Amphora

Answers on page 95

BROTHERS QUIZ

There are many pairs of brothers in the Bible. Draw a line to match the brother on the right with his brother on the left.

1	Cain	John
2	Isaac	Aaron
3	Esau	Benjamin
4	Ham	Abel
5	Peter	Shem
6	James	Andrew
7	Joseph	Ishmael
8	Moses	Jacob

Answers on page 95

CHURCH COUNCILS

Councils are meetings of the leaders of the Church in order to dialogue about serious issues or widespread problems. There are many different types of councils.

W	N	U	L	N	L	X	J	O	S	Y	T	N	T	C	R
O	A	B	A	P	F	A	S	E	R	U	O	N	H	I	C
R	R	M	I	J	G	Y	C	A	R	D	S	R	E	A	F
L	E	T	C	S	U	O	N	I	E	U	I	E	R	R	L
D	T	T	N	H	H	E	B	C	N	S	S	D	H	Y	T
W	A	K	I	J	L	O	L	Y	T	E	I	A	O	P	R
I	L	X	V	P	A	A	P	O	T	N	M	N	L	F	E
D	R	W	O	Z	H	I	L	Z	A	D	S	U	U	E	H
E	K	G	R	C	U	O	Q	L	Q	A	G	C	C	U	M
I	J	W	P	V	G	C	O	N	S	T	A	N	C	E	O
Z	V	A	T	I	C	A	N	A	E	A	C	I	N	Z	D
R	N	D	C	E	V	L	A	N	J	D	H	E	A	G	I
K	W	A	K	N	I	H	Z	B	N	L	I	P	V	B	L
E	L	P	O	N	I	T	N	A	T	S	N	O	C	U	G
N	H	W	G	E	A	I	F	E	S	D	P	P	W	C	U
E	C	N	E	R	O	L	F	H	B	C	M	H	Z	Z	H

Answers on page 84

BISHOP	CONSTANTINOPLE	LATERAN	PROVINCIAL
CARDINAL	ECUMENICAL	LYONS	TRENT
CHALCEDON	EPHESUS	NICAEA	VATICAN
CHRISTOLOGICAL	FLORENCE	PLENARY	VIENNE
CONSTANCE	JERUSALEM	POPE	WORLDWIDE

SAINT AUGUSTINE OF HIPPO

Saint Augustine was a Father of the Church and is said to have been one of the most influential Catholic writers in the history of the Church.

ADEODATUS BISHOP CITY OF GOD DIALOGUE

AFRICA CARTHAGE CONFESSIONS FOURTH CENTURY

AMBROSE CELIBACY CONVERSION HIPPO

MILAN

MONICA

ORIGINAL SIN

PELAGIANISM

PLATO

RHETORIC

ROMANS

TAGASTE

WESTERN FATHER

WRITER

Y	L	J	E	C	I	R	O	T	E	H	R	J	M	A	B
R	T	A	G	A	S	T	E	F	Q	T	M	L	T	K	V
U	E	R	C	R	C	O	N	V	E	R	S	I	O	N	M
T	K	H	I	T	M	R	T	W	S	A	M	R	E	A	S
N	W	U	T	H	H	I	P	P	O	U	C	D	N	U	T
E	R	D	Y	A	W	G	B	I	R	W	R	I	T	E	R
C	M	J	O	G	F	I	S	Y	B	O	C	A	R	V	I
H	W	F	F	E	S	N	C	J	M	H	D	L	V	F	N
T	K	P	G	H	K	A	R	A	A	O	F	O	X	J	A
R	O	O	O	S	B	L	N	E	E	S	H	G	G	D	L
U	F	P	D	I	A	S	N	D	T	X	Z	U	M	P	I
O	P	E	L	A	G	I	A	N	I	S	M	E	O	L	M
F	F	E	P	A	S	N	O	I	S	S	E	F	N	O	C
B	C	B	J	M	T	E	O	F	K	K	V	W	I	D	H
I	A	B	D	I	Q	O	Q	R	K	W	V	M	C	X	Q
X	M	Q	R	J	Q	W	G	G	I	S	X	S	A	U	Y

Answers on page 84

CROSSWORD PUZZLE NO. 5

ACROSS

1 Torah
4 To's partner
8 Milk and butter org.
11 First woman, and others
13 Water-resistant paper
14 Kind of complex
16 In favor of
17 "...he will come to judge the living and the _____"
18 Book of the Bible
20 Condition of Paul after his experience on the road to Damascus
22 Bishop's headdress
23 Site of first miracle
24 *Regina* _____
26 Excavate
27 Liturgical color for Christmas
28 Period of history
30 An instrument of the violin family
31 What God made the first man from
33 The patriarchs probably appreciated finding this in the desert
34 Jesus is the Prince of _____
35 Saint Peter _____
37 "You are the _____ of the earth" (Mt 5:13)
38 "_____ Father"
39 Vatican chapel
42 Frenzied
43 Saturate
44 Gave food
45 Jamaican popular music
46 Born, of a woman

DOWN

1 One of "the Great" popes
2 _____ *Maria*
3 Jesus' parable, The _____ Banquet
5 _____ to Emmaus
6 What biblical kings were anointed with
7 Chosen by Jesus
8 Legendary garden fruit
9 Navigational device
10 Got up
12 Saint Catherine of _____
15 Cushion
18 Vatican sculpture
19 Jackie O's hubby
20 Alphabet string
21 Pertaining to nonordained members of the Church
22 Posts
24 Church singers
25 Bric-a-_____
27 Magi
28 Joy
29 Affirmative vote
30 Sixth letter of the Hebrew alphabet
31 They were converted by Saint Patrick
32 Deride
33 Paddled
34 Step in ballet
36 Decoy
37 "Cure the ___, raise the dead, cleanse the lepers, cast out demons." (Mt 10:8)
39 Sibling, fondly
40 Not, in Scotland
41 Supplement

Answers on page 73

SACRAMENT TEST

Fill in the blanks from the clues below.

```
        S _ _ _
        _ A _ _ _ _ _
  _ _ _ _ C _ _ _ _ _ _ _
  _ _ _ _ R _ _ _ _ _
    _ _ _ A _ _ _ _
        M _ _ _ _ _ _ _
  _ _ _ _ _ _ E _ _
  _ _ _ _ _ _ N _ _ _ _ _ _ _
        _ _ _ _ T
```

A sacrament is an outward _____.

This sacrament makes you a member of the Church.

This sacrament is the offer of God's forgiveness.

This sacrament was originally received along with baptism.

This is the central sacrament.

This sacrament binds a man and a woman as a couple.

This is a sacrament of vocation.

This is a sacrament of healing.

The Sacrament of God.

Answers on page 95

CRYPTOGRAM NO. 4

In this sentence, letters have been substituted for other letters. For example, "DJS DLAS JWM BQAS" is "THE TIME HAS COME." The words are in their correct order, with a space after each word. You can break the code by watching for the frequency of certain letters or the way letters are grouped. A single letter is usually "A" or "I." Groupings of two may be "it," "by," or "of," for example. This cryptogram is a common Bible phrase or catechism answer.

SEAO PETV BCOO LB ZTEFU ISU OLTY AN KAIS ISUU.

Answers on page 95

CROSSWORD PUZZLE NO. 6

ACROSS

1 "_____ and female he created them." (Gen 1:27)
4 _____ Gennesaret
7 Mother of Mary
8 Old Testament book (abbr.)
9 Secure
13 Dell
15 Salaries
17 Writers and interpreters of the Jewish law
18 Greatest king of Israel
19 "..._____, lema sabachthani?" (Mt 27:46)
21 _____ of Galilee
22 _____ homo
23 One of the symbols on the papal flag
24 Again
26 Victuals
28 Holy ones (abbr.)
29 Tribe of Israel
31 Explorer, Blessed Junipero _____
34 Three visitors
36 "...thy _____ come, thy will be done..."
39 Not fer
40 Land of Saint Patrick
41 Ike's initials
42 Theologial degree (abbr.)
43 Cravats
44 Hard fatty tissue

DOWN

1 Another name for 34A
2 Pertaining to nonordained members of the Church
3 Dignify
4 Members of the priestly caste of Judaism
5 Evil king of Israel
6 Sheep
10 Besides
11 Liturgical color of Pentecost
12 Religious instruction classes
14 Thirteen popes
16 Secure
17 Sacrament of the _____
20 Holy images
21 Church council
24 Is present at, as a liturgy
25 Small bird
26 Utensil
27 Knives
30 Hairpiece
31 The Red or the Dead
32 Help
33 One of two New Testament books (abbr.)
34 "The Lord is my shepherd, I shall not ___" (Ps 23:1)
35 Soldiers pierced Jesus' ___ when he was on the cross
37 "God," in Marseilles
38 What we abstain from on certain Fridays

Answers on page 73

INSIDE THE CHURCH BUILDING

Catholic church buildings have been the receptacles of much great artwork over the years. A tour of a Catholic church can do much to enhance one's understanding of Catholicism.

Word list		
ALTAR		
AMBRY		
ANTEPENDIUM		
APSE		
BALDACCHINO		
BAPTISMAL FONT		
BAPTISTERY		
CANDLE		
CATHEDRA		
CERECLOTH		
CHANCEL		
CHAPEL		
CHOIR		
COMMUNION RAIL		
CRUCIFIX		
DOSSAL		
FRONTAL	PEW	SEDILIA
ICON	PULPIT	SHRINE
KNEELER	REREDOS	STAINED GLASS
LECTERN	SACRISTY	TABERNACLE
NAVE	SANCTUARY	VESTIBULE

```
A D Y R B M A I J A W W A B V E
E C H M U I D N E P E T N A S H
N H J H L Q G T T I P L U P S L
I A Q I E L C A N R E B A T H V
R P D O S S A L T A R D A I E B
H E C H A N C E L U B I T S E V
S L N L I A R N O I N U M M O C
G D B A P T I S T E R Y C A J N
V N E C A T H E D R A H Q L Z G
S A F N C V W G C R U C I F I X
O C R H T O L C E R E C S O C D
D D O A B A L D A C C H I N O J
E I N F S A N C T U A R Y T N C
R Y T S I R C A S L E C T E R N
E Q A C H H W G V P E B D Q F W
R E L E E N K P F E A Y Y N F M
```

Answers on page 84

KINGS OF ISRAEL & JUDAH

Israel was a united country from about 1000 BC until about 900 BC. About 900 BC a civil war divided the country into two parts that became known as Israel and Judah.

ABIJAM AHAZIAH BAASHA HEZEKIAH JEHOSHAPHAT

AHAB ASA DAVID HOSHEA JEROBOAM

AHAZ AZARIAH ELAH JEHORAM JOASH

JOSIAH

MENAHEM

NADAB

OMRI

PEKAH

REHOBOAM

SAUL

SHALLUM

SOLOMON

ZEDEKIAH

ZIMRI

```
D  Z  V  H  A  I  G  H  Q  M  R  Y  M  S  M
A  B  A  A  S  H  A  I  D  A  M  I  W  O  A
E  P  O  I  J  I  A  I  R  A  H  Y  O  L  J
H  N  T  T  K  T  V  Z  O  M  Y  A  M  O  I
S  A  Y  E  G  A  K  B  I  V  I  V  R  M  B
O  Q  Z  E  D  B  O  A  A  A  Q  Z  I  O  A
H  E  L  M  A  R  O  H  E  J  H  Y  J  N  H
H  A  C  R  E  L  M  A  O  B  O  H  E  R  A
H  Y  B  J  E  F  Y  A  Z  A  R  I  A  H  M
Z  E  D  E  K  I  A  H  N  A  D  A  B  K  U
F  P  E  K  A  H  V  Y  R  B  Y  P  C  U  L
A  T  A  H  P  A  H  S  O  H  E  J  F  L  L
H  S  M  X  M  E  H  A  N  E  M  J  S  Q  A
L  U  A  S  E  N  L  P  S  Z  K  L  A  E  H
H  A  I  S  O  J  O  A  S  H  K  M  B  S  S
```

Answers on page 85

HIDDEN BOOKS

In each of the sentences below, the name of a book of the Bible appears. It is hidden within the words of the sentence. For example, in the sentence "When Bill's car went in a rut, he had to call for a tow truck," the Book of RUTH is hidden (...in a RUT, He had...). Find the Bible book in each sentence.

1   We often have to teach young children not to bite.

2   Since Susan was the tallest, her basketball coach had her play center.

3   How is Dominic doing since the operation?

4   I try not to do much work on a humid day.

5   Since Joe left his mitt at home, he couldn't play ball.

6   I was thinking, should she go out without a coat on this cold day?

7   Joe likes strong tea, so he brews it a long time.

8   What kind of mark did you get on your test?

9   The teacher's pet erases the board for her.

10   There used to be a movie review show starring Gene Siskel and Roger Ebert.

Answers on page 95

WOMEN OF THE BIBLE

See if you can name the women in the Bible who fit the following descriptions.

1   She was one of the first people to find Jesus' tomb empty on Easter morning.

2   She saved the Jews from the evil plot of Haman.

3   She watched out for her brother as he lay in a basket floating down the Nile.

4   She saved the Jews from the attack of the Assyrians.

5   She sat at Jesus' feet to learn from him while her sister did housework.

6   She danced so well that Herod agreed to kill John the Baptist at her request.

7   She was an evil queen, eaten by dogs at her death.

Answers on page 95

LITURGY

Liturgy means "work of the people." It refers to all forms of prayer.

ACCLAMATION

ANAMNESIS

BLESSING

COMMUNION

CONSECRATION

CREED

DISMISSAL

DOXOLOGY

EPICLESIS

EUCHARISTIC

FAITHFUL

GESTURE

GLORIA

GOSPEL

HOMILY

HOURS

INTERCESSION

INTRODUCTORY RITE

R	F	S	N	E	A	O	B	X	N	D	D	Y	P	S	O	S	V
I	Q	C	P	O	L	C	L	R	O	F	F	E	R	T	O	R	Y
X	N	I	D	E	I	A	C	X	I	S	O	E	E	E	O	S	W
N	R	T	P	I	U	S	O	L	T	S	Y	M	P	R	A	I	O
D	O	S	R	T	S	L	S	F	A	A	B	I	A	C	C	G	R
T	O	I	I	O	O	M	A	E	R	M	C	W	R	Z	E	N	D
G	H	R	N	G	D	I	I	P	C	L	A	A	A	S	U	O	X
S	O	A	Y	U	T	U	G	S	E	R	M	T	T	B	G	F	S
O	U	H	N	H	M	N	C	S	S	E	E	U	I	F	S	P	Y
L	R	C	F	K	I	M	I	T	N	A	R	T	O	O	G	E	R
E	S	U	B	N	S	S	O	T	O	E	L	B	N	L	N	A	A
M	L	E	E	B	G	G	A	C	C	R	M	J	O	I	I	C	N
N	K	P	E	Q	L	R	I	Z	E	A	Y	R	F	J	D	E	O
H	O	M	I	L	Y	Z	G	V	L	F	I	R	G	G	A	Q	I
T	P	E	N	I	T	E	N	T	I	A	L	R	I	T	E	S	T
A	W	O	S	I	S	E	N	M	A	N	A	T	F	T	R	I	C
P	R	X	U	B	L	E	S	S	I	N	G	U	T	O	E	W	E
E	S	N	O	P	S	E	R	E	Y	A	R	P	S	D	R	O	L

LAMB OF GOD	OFFERTORY	READINGS	SIGN OF PEACE
LECTIONARY	OPENING PRAYER	RESPONSE	SOLEMN
LORD'S PRAYER	PENITENTIAL RITE	RITUAL	THANKSGIVING
MASS		SACRAMENTARY	WORD
	PREPARATION OF GIFTS		

Answers on page 86

THE APOCALYPSE

Revelation is the last book of the New Testament. Highly symbolic and cryptic, it talks of the end of time.

ANGEL

BABYLON

BEAST

BOWL

CHRIST

CHURCHES

DRAGON

HARVEST OF THE EARTH

HEAVENLY WORSHIP

INTERLUDES

JERUSALEM

JOHN

KING OF KINGS

LAMB OF GOD

LAST BOOK

MULTITUDE

```
H  Q  I  L  N  L  P  T  X  N  Y  G  T  T  S  G  H  N
X  A  A  N  L  O  R  L  E  X  N  L  H  X  G  E  E  E
C  E  R  O  T  U  I  W  A  O  R  O  P  E  N  D  A  W
S  H  R  V  M  E  H  T  S  G  U  J  B  N  I  K  V  E
R  C  U  P  E  E  R  Y  A  S  U  O  C  O  K  L  E  A
S  J  E  R  A  S  R  L  A  V  R  E  H  I  F  A  N  R
L  T  N  V  C  O  T  N  U  E  L  S  R  S  O  M  L  T
N  E  E  O  T  H  D  O  T  D  S  A  I  I  G  B  Y  H
G  N  G  C  I  Y  E  I  F  E  E  F  S  V  N  O  W  Q
R  B  I  N  E  T  H  S  V  T  F  S  T  T  I  F  O  E
H  V  S  A  A  W  A  E  X  V  H  Y  H  W  K  G  R  D
I  D  R  A  G  O  N  E  I  M  S  E  I  B  H  O  S  U
S  S  N  O  I  T  C  E  R  R  U  S  E  R  S  D  H  T
M  E  L  A  S  U  R  E  J  C  W  B  E  A  X  T  I  I
L  A  S  T  B  O  O  K  B  O  W  L  B  N  R  Z  P  T
W  H  I  T  E  T  H  R  O  N  E  E  Y  H  T  T  N  L
N  O  L  Y  B  A  B  T  S  A  E  B  N  O  O  I  H  U
H  X  B  Q  D  F  Y  X  Y  I  H  F  B  J  B  Z  W  M
```

NEW CREATION

NEW EARTH

NEW HEAVEN

PLAGUE

RESURRECTION

SALVATION

SCROLL

SEAL

SEVEN

THOUSAND YEARS

TRUMPET

VICTORY SONG

VISION

WHITE ROBE

WHITE THRONE

WITNESS

Answers on page 87

JUGGLED SAINTS

Elizabeth made saint flashcards to help her study for a test. She cut the cards in half and juggled them to test herself. See if you can correctly rematch the names.

Michael of Padua   _____

Rose Borromeo   _____

Teresa Alacoque   _____

John Loyola   _____

Catherine Kolbe   _____

Peter of Arc   _____

Frances the Archangel   _____

Anthony Claver   _____

Julian Cabrini   _____

Ignatius of Siena   _____

Francis Vianney   _____

Charles of Norwich   _____

Margaret Mary of Lima   _____

Joan of Avila   _____

Maximilian of Assisi   _____

Answers on page 95

CROSSWORD FILL-IN NO. 4

DIRECTIONS

Answers for this puzzle are listed below. Across and Down words are mixed together. Find each word's correct position in the cross-word grid. Some three-letter words are abbreviations.

3 LETTERS	**4 LETTERS**	**5 LETTERS**	**6 LETTERS**	**7 LETTERS**	**8 LETTERS**
PHM	PIUS	PACEM	PASTOR	PROPHET	ST. PETER'S
PIO	POPE	PAPAL	PRAGUE	REQUIEM	
PYX	SAUL	POPES	REPENT		
RAM	SETH	SHEEP	SAMSON		
RED	SONG	SLOTH	SERMON		
ROM		SONGS	SPIRIT		
SEE		ST. PAT	ST. PIUS		
SIX		STRAW			
STE		SWISS			
STS		TEMPT			
TEN					

Answers on page 74

THE MIDDLE AGES

The years AD 1000–1500 were the Middle Ages. It was a time of great devotion and piety. It was also the period during which the Eastern and Western churches split.

ARCHITECTURE

ART

BERNARD OF CLAIRVAUX

CANOSSA

CATHEDRAL

CHRISTENDOM

COLLEGE OF CARDINALS

COUNCIL OF CONSTANCE

CRUSADES

DOMINIC GUZMAN

EAST-WEST SCHISM

EXCOMMUNICATION

FRANCIS OF ASSISI

HILDEBRAND

INNOCENT III

INTERDICT

JOAN OF ARC

LATERAN COUNCIL

MENDICANT

MICHAEL CERULARIUS

MIDDLE AGES

MYSTERY PLAY

ORTHODOX CHURCH

PEACE OF GOD

PHILOSOPHY

PIETY

PRAYER CARVED IN STONE

RELIC

RENAISSANCE

THOMAS A BECKET

THOMAS AQUINAS

TRANSUBSTANTIATION

TRUCE OF GOD

WESTERN SCHISM

```
S E G A E L D D I M C H R I S T E N D O M
A N M J Y M S I H C S T S E W T S A E R Y
N O I T A C I N U M M O C X E R I D M T S
I T C C D O M I N I C G U Z M A N J T H T
U S H O L A R D E H T A C Q Y N T M Z O E
Q N A U L M S I H C S N R E T S E W T D R
A I E N D L A V T T L L U W E U R B R O Y
S D L C I L E R W G F I S O I B D W U X P
A E C I F D O G F O E C A E P S I Q C C L
M V E L T J S S E F D N D H M T C N E H A
O R R O Q R S W R O R U E U S A T D O U Y
H A U F I S I S S A F O S I C N A R F R C
T C L C O R M E N D I C A N T T T G G C A
T R A O D C C R A F O N A O J I Z F O H N
B E R N A R D O F C L A I R V A U X D K O
U Y I S Q H I L D E B R A N D T J V J U S
N A U T V A I N N O C E N T I I I H B H S
O R S A R C H I T E C T U R E O N W Y D A
C P Q N R E N A I S S A N C E N X A U O Y
V O V C R Y H P O S O L I H P G Q T L N E
U S T E K C E B A S A M O H T P G Z I S L
```

Answers on page 88

MISSIONARIES & EXPLORERS

The Catholic countries of Spain and France sent many explorers and missionaries to the Americas. Missionary work has been a tradition in the Church since its inception.

ALLOUEZ

ALTHAM

AUGUSTINE

BADIN

BONIFACE

BREBEUF

CHAMPLAIN

COLUMBUS

DAMIEN

DE LEON

DE NIZA

DE PADILLA

DE SOTO

DOUAY

FOUCAULT

FRANCIS
XAVIER

GOUPIL

M	O	R	E	N	O	W	H	I	T	E	A	P	S
L	I	P	U	O	G	M	D	E	N	I	Z	A	E
F	R	A	N	C	I	S	X	A	V	I	E	R	U
C	O	L	U	M	B	U	S	M	E	Y	U	B	G
S	J	T	O	G	T	L	U	A	C	U	O	F	O
E	J	H	N	D	U	B	A	D	I	N	L	E	J
G	B	A	A	N	E	S	J	S	I	O	L	O	P
H	X	M	Z	Y	X	P	T	F	A	I	A	A	D
E	C	H	A	M	P	L	A	I	N	L	T	E	E
R	E	U	R	X	X	C	M	D	N	R	L	S	S
S	O	Q	R	C	E	D	A	M	I	E	N	E	O
D	B	R	E	B	E	U	F	C	O	L	T	R	T
X	S	H	V	O	N	I	K	N	H	F	L	R	O
H	J	O	L	I	E	T	T	E	U	Q	R	A	M

JOGUES

JOLIET

KINO

LA SALLE

MARQUETTE

MORENO

PATRICK

POLO

SEGHERS

SERRA

VERRAZANO

WHITE

Answers on page 89

CROSSWORD PUZZLE NO. 7

ACROSS

1 "Let anyone among you who is without ____ be the first ..." (Jn 8:7)
4 ___ Wednesday
6 Charlemagne was emperor of this Christian kingdom (abbr.)
9 Middle Easterner
10 False god of the Old Testament
11 Taxi
12 Basketball great with an M.D.?
14 Naught, nothing
15 What lectors do at Mass
17 Rosary ____
18 Rule
20 Look
22 Minor prophet
24 "Take, ___..." (Mt 26:26)
26 Sorrowful
29 Hosea's wife
31 Jubilee _____
33 A vestment
34 What Abraham sacrificed in place of Isaac
35 First patriarch, to his friends?
36 Veronica's ____
37 English public school
38 Superlative ending
39 Mother of Mary
40 Humble dwelling

DOWN

1 ___ *Coeur*
2 *Dies* _____
3 David married his widow
5 Inhabitant of Eastern Europe
6 Laying on of _____
7 Jesus ___ Lazarus from the dead
8 Former measure of length
13 The Incarnation
16 Tribe of Israel
19 Communion host
21 "I bore you up on ____ wings." (Ex 19:4)
23 Month of Mary
25 Old Testament book
27 "Dying you destroyed our _____"
28 Major sixteeth-century council of the Church
30 There were forty days and nights of this in Genesis
32 ____ ben Adhem
33 _____ *Maria*

Answers on page 73

JUGGLED CATHOLIC TERMS

Elizabeth made flashcards of two-word Catholic terms to help her study for a test. She cut the cards in half and juggled them to test herself. See if you can correctly rematch the names.

Roman Commandments   _____

Holy Domini   _____

Last Wednesday   _____

Old Sins   _____

Ten Judgment   _____

Beloved Days   _____

Ash Office   _____

Capital Testament   _____

Canon Disciple   _____

Anno Council   _____

Divine See   _____

Ecumenical Grace   _____

Feast Rail   _____

Sanctifying Pontiff   _____

Communion Law   _____

Answers on page 96

U.S. CITIES WITH CATHEDRALS

A cathedral is a diocesan church and the bishop's "chair." It is usually located in the "see city" from which the diocese takes its name.

ALLENTOWN

AUSTIN

BALTIMORE

BATON ROUGE

BIRMINGHAM

BOISE

COLUMBUS

CROOKSTON

DAVENPORT

DES MOINES

DODGE CITY

EVANSVILLE

FORT WAYNE

GARY

GRAND RAPIDS

GREEN BAY

HARTFORD

JUNEAU

KNOXVILLE

LAS CRUCES

LOUISVILLE

MONTEREY

NEW ORLEANS

OMAHA

ORLANDO

PARMA

ROCKFORD

SAN DIEGO

SANTA FE

SAVANNAH

SPRINGFIELD

STOCKTON

TRENTON

WASHINGTON, D.C.

YAKIMA

```
Q E A U S T I N L A M R A P P W T
Y F W H G W A S H I N G T O N D C
Y A L F E N Y A W T R O F T F Y Z
T T B A U A T S N A E L R O W E N
I N S N S P R I N G F I E L D R O
C A W A E C L D U O M A H A A E T
E S S O V E R O M I T L A B V T N
G L C D T A R U U S N S G A E N E
D U L N P N N G C I T P K J N O R
O E S I O B E N Y E S O G O P M T
D V D T V I Q L A A S V C A O X H
N S A V Q S N X L H K Z I K R R Q
A B I R M I N G H A M I Q L T Y C
L O G E I D N A S S U B M U L O C
R Q U F E L L I V X O N K A Y E N
O H A R T F O R D E S M O I N E S
D R O F K C O R J U N E A U S V Q
```

Answers on page 89

BIBLICAL WORDS & PHRASES

CAST THE
FIRST STONE

LABOR OF
LOVE

NO RESPECTER
OF PERSONS

NO REST FOR
THE WICKED

OLIVE
BRANCH

PATIENCE
OF JOB

PHILISTINE

POOR AS JOB

RAISE CAIN

SCAPEGOAT

SEE HOW THE
LAND LIES

STILL SMALL
VOICE

SUFFER FOOLS
GLADLY

```
Q S Z B A E C I O V L L A M S L L I T S R
I G S E I T I N A V F O Y T I N A V W S D
N N U C A S T T H E F I R S T S T O N E O
T I F N I S F O S E G A W P M E P O K N C
V H F T V F M J O L I Y O U E A S C T R S
Z T E K U M T M D S D O V T T R I Q W E D
W Y R S S R D Q E U R L H I E W Q N I D N
I R F C W N N C R A G S E P E Y M L N L A
S E O A G E A T S I E N F H R U D A K I H
D V O P B I A J H T C O T O Y N E B L W S
O E L E N X O T O E R R L E A X N O I E E
M R S G P B R N O E O I U L M Y I R N H N
O O G O R Y E F T F V T E U T C T O G T O
F F L A K D J C T E Y H H T G V S F O N G
S E A T G O E S B R T O W E P A I L F I N
O M D E B P E R P W L P U T R M L O A E I
L I L Z S R A V O W Y N W R I C I V N C H
O T Y E O N L H Q R N A N P B F H E E I S
M X R N C G E F D A K Q O B W R P E Y O A
O O A H S E L F L L A F O Y A W O L E V W
N G V L S J D O O L B G N I T A E W S K J
```

SWEATING
BLOOD

TEETH SET
ON EDGE

THE SWEAT OF
YOUR BROW

TIME FOR
EVERYTHING

TURN THE
OTHER CHEEK

TWINKLING
OF AN EYE

VANITY OF VANITIES

VOICE IN THE
WILDERNESS

WAGES OF SIN

WASHING
ONE'S HANDS

WAY OF
ALL FLESH

WISDOM OF
SOLOMON

Answers on page 90

CATHEDRAL CITIES

ALEXANDRIA

ATLANTA

BROOKLYN

CHARLOTTE

CHEYENNE

COLORADO SPRINGS

COVINGTON

DALLAS

DETROIT

EL PASO

FALL RIVER

HONOLULU

JEFFERSON CITY

LA CROSSE

LAFAYETTE

LEXINGTON

MADISON

METUCHEN

MIAMI

NEWTON

OKLAHOMA CITY

PHILADELPHIA

PITTSBURGH

RALEIGH

ROCHESTER

SAN ANGELO

SAN ANTONIO

SAN JOSE

TUCSON

WILMINGTON

```
C Y R E V I R L L A F A Y E T T E
N O T G N I X E L P A S O L I D S
H M L I U D M E T U C H E N O M S
R D P O C Z X Y I F O S G B R G O
X U P H R A H C R I V W J W T L R
S O Q H N A M H N E N N E Y E H C
A Y J D I O D O G N T N F A D J A
L D R H Z L T O H R S S F X C H L
L I W O G N A G S A U N E W T O N
A T P U A I N D N P L B R H C H C
D U M N L E E A E I R K S E C E N
B C A K M U N L T L V I O T X O Z
Q S D X M G L A A N P O N J T M R
J O I J E T T O L R A H C G Q I T
R N S L N O T G N I M L I W S A P
B R O O K L Y N K O F F T A X M D
S A N J O S E W Z P H G Y A K I G
```

Answers on page 91

PAPAL MATCH-UP

How much do you know about the papacy? Test your knowledge below. Choices are at the bottom of the page, or see how many you know without looking at the choices.

1   The name of the enclosure of cardinals to elect a pope _____

2   This begins for a pope when he accepts election _____

3   A symbol of papal office _____ _____

4   The director of the conclave that elects the pope _____

5   This is a letter, usually on doctrine, written by a pope _____

6   A solemn, formal document issued regarding serious matters _____

7   Religious order that oversees the papal radio station _____

8   Religious order that provides the papal theologian (Master of the Sacred Palace) _____

9   Annual universal collection to help defray the cost of a pope's expenses _____

10 Summer residence of the pope _____

Select from this list:

Bull	Dominican
Castel Gandolfo	Encyclical
Chamberlain	Jesuit
Conclave	Peter's Pence
Crossed Keys	Pontificate

Answers on page 96

CRYPTOGRAM NO. 5

In this sentence letters have been substituted for other letters. For example, "DJS DLAS JWM BQAS" is "THE TIME HAS COME." The words are in their correct order, with a space after each word. You can break the code by watching for the frequency of certain letters or the way letters are grouped. A single letter is usually "A" or "I." Groupings of two may be "it," "by," or "of," for example. This cryptogram is a common Bible phrase or catechism answer.

OT QC EZQWE DTGZBT RZF JZ EXAQATT; JOTBT RZF

HQAA CTT OQY, XC OT JZAU RZF.

Answers on page 96

69

OLD TESTAMENT EVENTS

Some of the most notable events in the Bible occurred in Old Testament times.

ARK LOST

CAPTURE OF LOT

EXILE

JOSEPH IN EGYPT

BATTLE OF JERICHO

CIVIL WAR

EXODUS

KINGDOM

COMMANDMENTS

FIRST SIN

MACCABEAN REVOLT

BIRTH OF MOSES

CREATION

GREEK INVASION

MURDER OF ABEL

CALL OF ABRAHAM

DESERT WANDERING

JACOB'S DECEIT

NOAH'S ARK

PARTING OF THE SEA

PASSOVER

PERIOD OF JUDGES

PROPHECY

RESTORATION

ROMAN OCCUPATION

TEMPLE

TOWER OF BABEL

```
B  T  E  M  P  L  E  C  A  Y  S  P  C  K  P  J  T  T
C  A  L  L  O  F  A  B  R  A  H  A  M  T  N  K  T  C
I  E  T  S  C  D  Y  C  E  H  P  O  R  P  O  B  I  A
T  S  F  T  S  E  G  D  U  J  F  O  D  O  I  R  E  P
L  E  I  N  L  S  M  N  C  O  T  T  M  R  T  A  C  T
E  H  R  E  V  E  D  U  I  R  I  S  T  G  A  W  E  U
B  T  S  M  S  R  O  F  R  K  E  H  J  R  P  L  D  R
A  F  T  D  T  T  A  F  X  D  O  A  K  P  U  I  S  E
B  O  S  N  K  W  G  A  J  F  E  L  T  E  C  V  B  O
F  G  I  A  J  A  W  T  M  E  O  R  L  I  C  I  O  F
O  N  N  M  I  N  H  O  Y  S  R  I  O  E  O  C  C  L
R  I  A  M  L  D  S  W  T  L  X  I  K  F  N  N  A  O
E  T  L  O  V  E  R  N  A  E  B  A  C  C  A  M  J  T
W  R  W  C  S  R  E  V  O  S  S  A  P  H  M  B  D  F
O  A  P  N  O  I  T  A  R  O  T  S  E  R  O  Y  E  F
T  P  Y  G  E  N  I  H  P  E  S  O  J  M  R  S  E  L
C  L  D  E  J  G  R  E  E  K  I  N  V  A  S  I  O  N
S  K  R  A  S  H  A  O  N  S  U  D  O  X  E  C  C  J
```

Answers on page 92

CROSSWORD PUZZLE SOLUTIONS

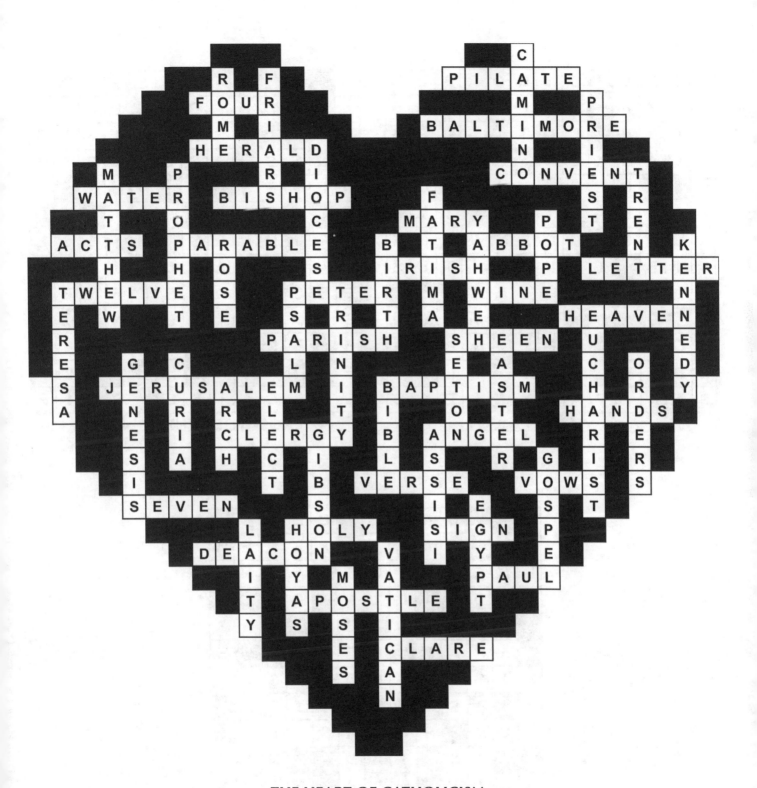

THE HEART OF CATHOLICISM

CROSSWORD PUZZLE SOLUTIONS

CROSSWORD PUZZLE NO. 2

```
A B E L   C I B O R I U M
H A Z E   A C E   E S S E
A A R E   L O T   A C E A
B L A C K E N   B R A   N
    H E B   N I M R O D
P A T E N   I O N   I T E
A M O S   C C D   M O O R
R I B   T H E   R I T E S
A D O N A I   L A C
B   G A D   R A P H A E L
L O G O   L E I   A B B A
E D A M   E A T   E L O I
S A N I T A R Y   L E N D
```

CROSSWORD PUZZLE NO. 3

```
B   P   T   A C E   M   P
A B E D N E G O   L O S E
R A T   T R A P P I S T S
U N E S   A P E   G E E K
C E R E S   E   I H S   Y
H   S T A R   E A T   O
  Q   H U E S   M   S S E
M A T   L A I C   J O E L
E D O M   D A R K E N E D
S I M O N   M E O W
H   B R A C   C A S T E L
E   A S H   H   E L O
S T B L A I S E   S N I P
```

CROSSWORD PUZZLE NO. 4

```
E   O N C E   O B E D
D A   F A I L   R E N E W
E D O M   T O E   A N N E
N O D   E I N   R U
  N O M A D   D T   I H S
  A R A M   D E B S   E
H I S S   C C D   E S S E
A   S A U L   I T C H
B V M   S R   A S H E R
  I N   I A M   N I B
A C T I   A L B   E T N A
D A R N S   E R A S   E T
  M E E T   C Y T E   E
```

CROSSWORD PUZZLE SOLUTIONS

CROSSWORD PUZZLE NO. 5

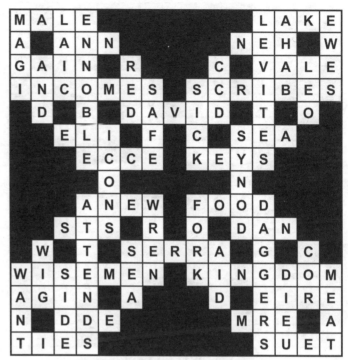

CROSSWORD PUZZLE NO. 6

CROSSWORD PUZZLE NO. 7

CROSSWORD FILL-IN PUZZLE SOLUTIONS

CROSSWORD FILL-IN NO. 1

CROSSWORD FILL-IN NO. 2

CROSSWORD FILL-IN NO. 3

CROSSWORD FILL-IN NO. 4

74

WORD SEARCH PUZZLE SOLUTIONS

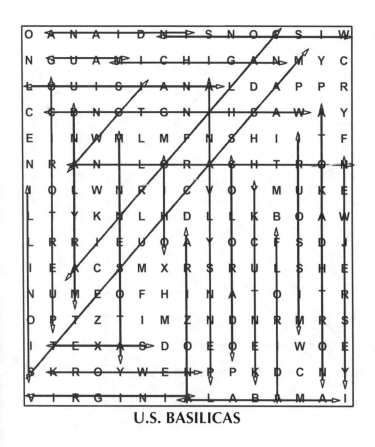

U.S. BASILICAS

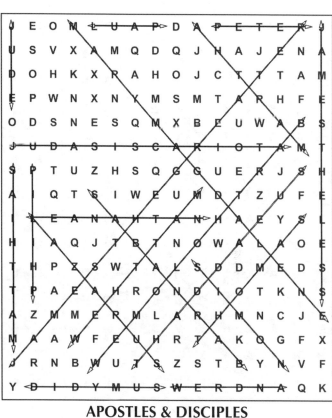

APOSTLES & DISCIPLES

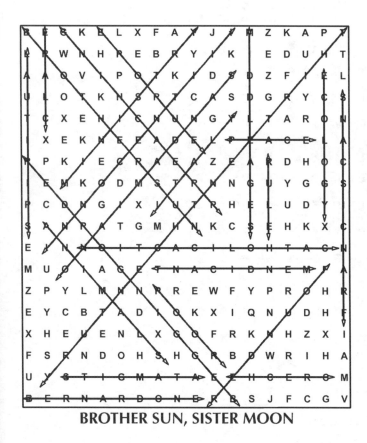

BROTHER SUN, SISTER MOON

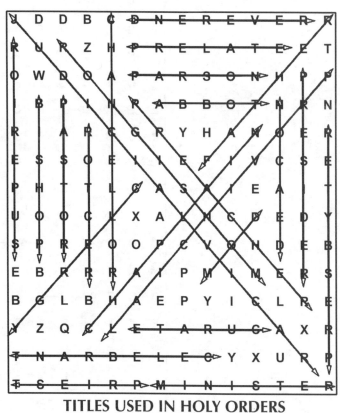

TITLES USED IN HOLY ORDERS

WORD SEARCH PUZZLE SOLUTIONS

THE CROSS

PROPHETICAL & HISTORICAL BOOKS

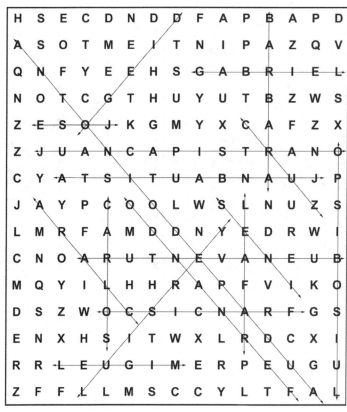

CALIFORNIA MISSIONS

WORD SEARCH PUZZLE SOLUTIONS

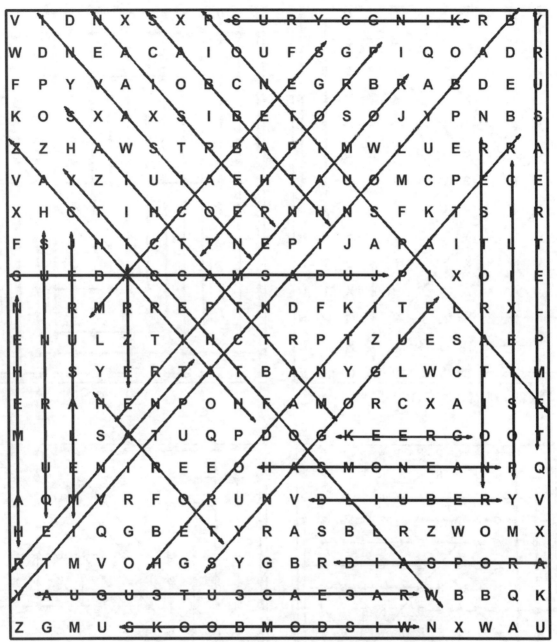

CAPTIVITY THROUGH POST-EXILIC PERIOD

WORD SEARCH PUZZLE SOLUTIONS

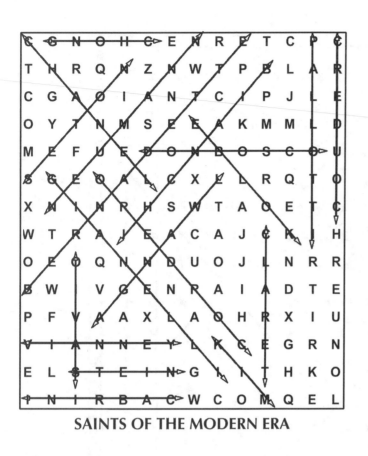

SAINTS OF THE MODERN ERA

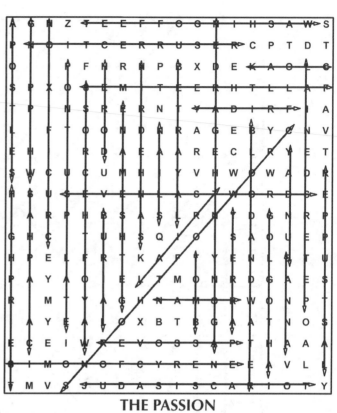

THE PASSION

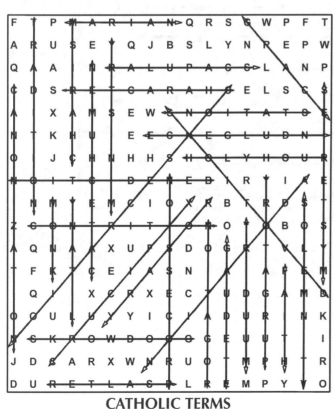

CATHOLIC TERMS

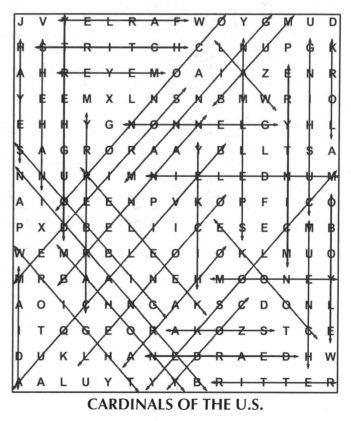

CARDINALS OF THE U.S.

WORD SEARCH PUZZLE SOLUTIONS

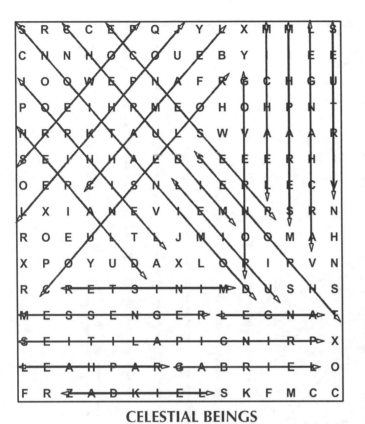

CELESTIAL BEINGS

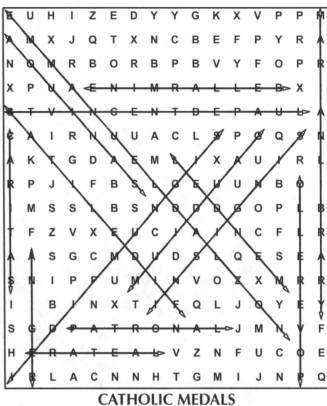

CATHOLIC MEDALS

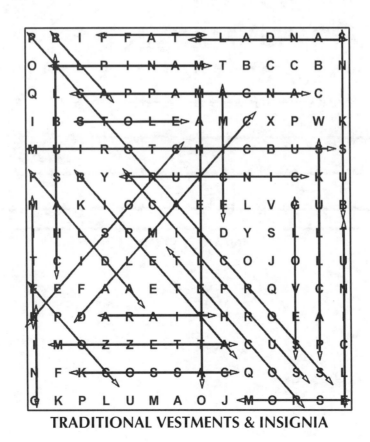

TRADITIONAL VESTMENTS & INSIGNIA

WORD SEARCH PUZZLE SOLUTIONS

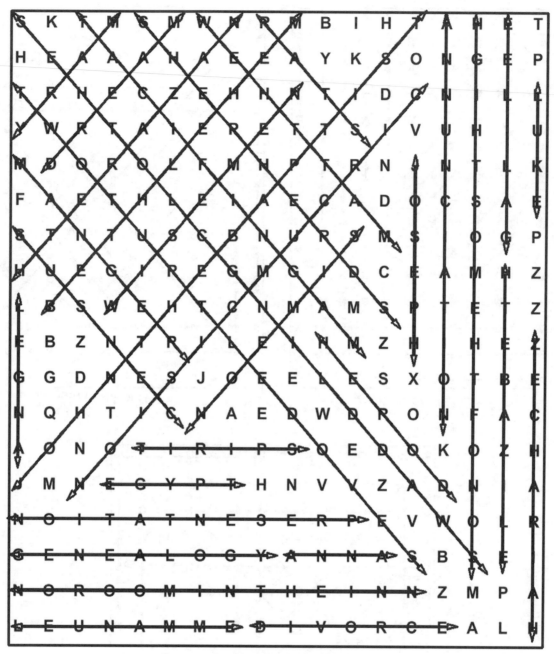

INFANCY STORIES

WORD SEARCH PUZZLE SOLUTIONS

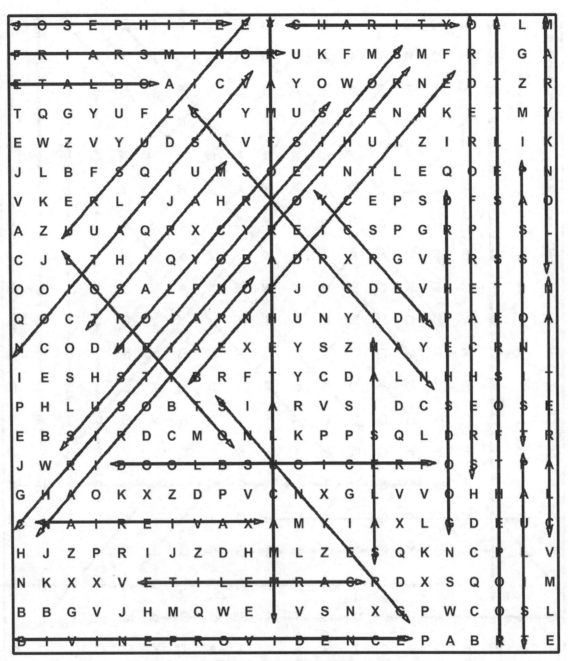

RELIGIOUS ORDERS

WORD SEARCH PUZZLE SOLUTIONS

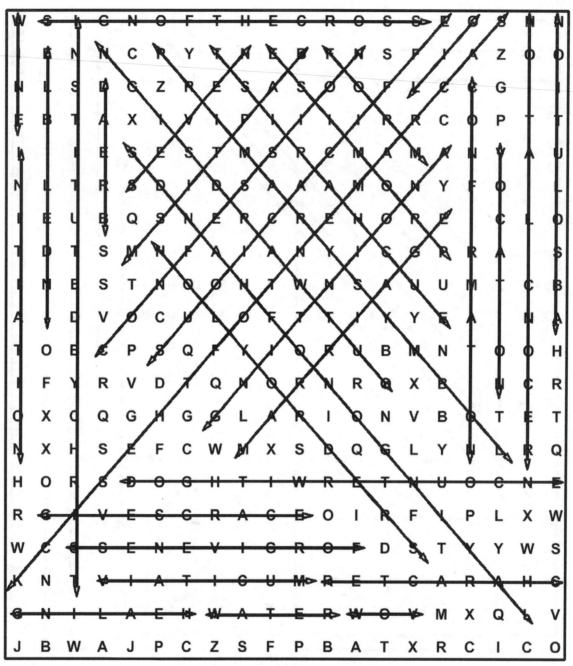

ENCOUNTERING GOD

WORD SEARCH PUZZLE SOLUTIONS

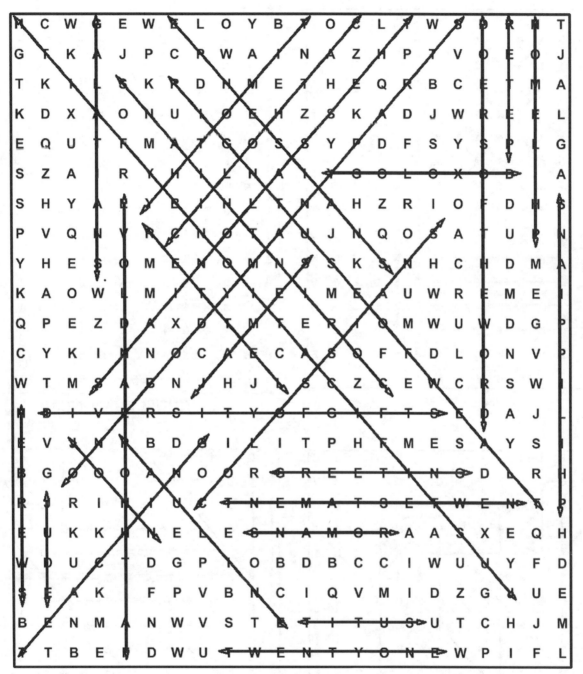

EPISTLES

WORD SEARCH PUZZLE SOLUTIONS

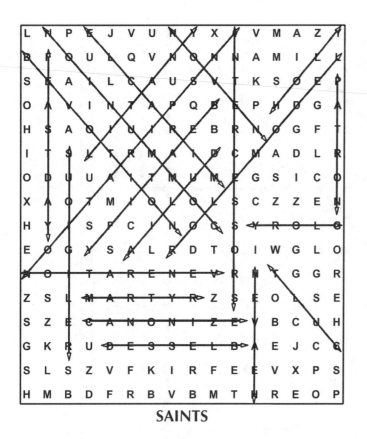

SAINTS

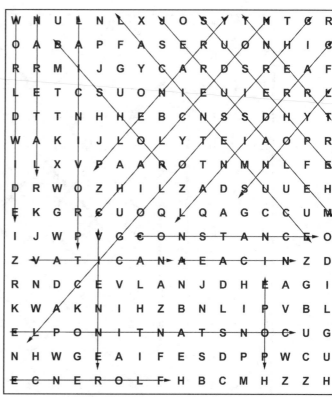

CHURCH COUNCILS

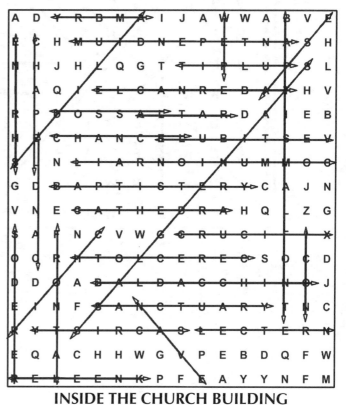

SAINT AUGUSTINE OF HIPPO

INSIDE THE CHURCH BUILDING

WORD SEARCH PUZZLE SOLUTIONS

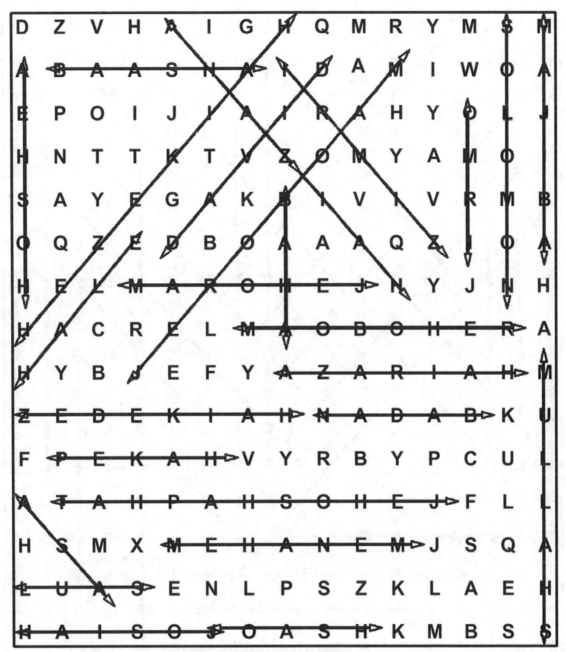

KINGS OF ISRAEL & JUDAH

WORD SEARCH PUZZLE SOLUTIONS

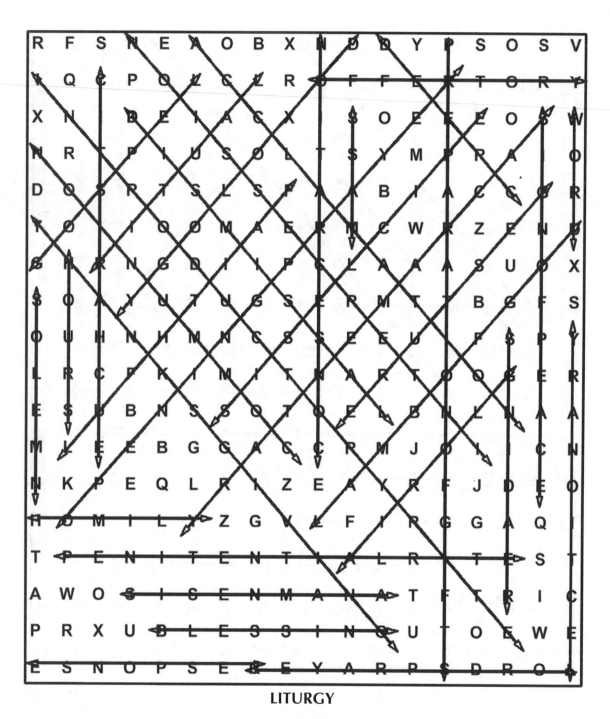

LITURGY

WORD SEARCH PUZZLE SOLUTIONS

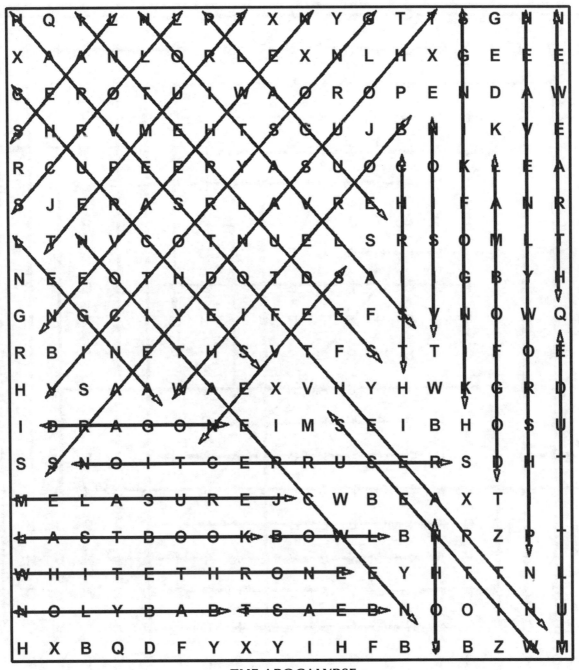

THE APOCALYPSE

WORD SEARCH PUZZLE SOLUTIONS

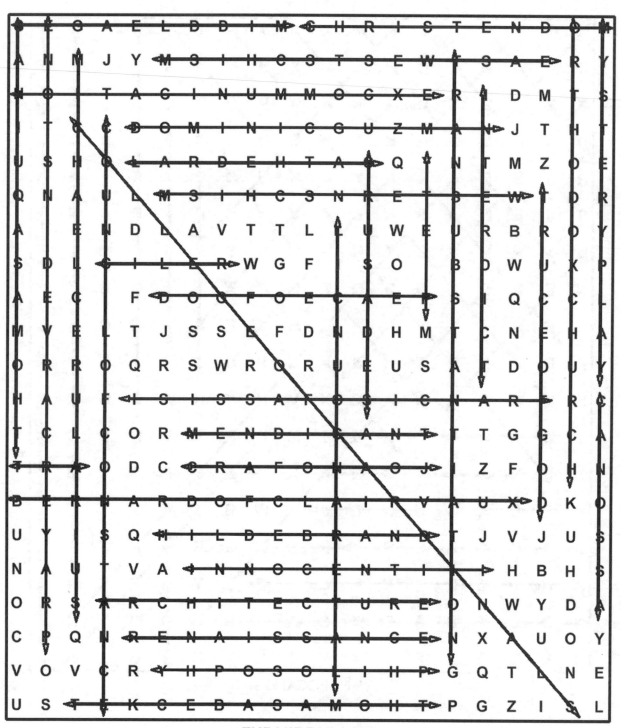

THE MIDDLE AGES

WORD SEARCH PUZZLE SOLUTIONS

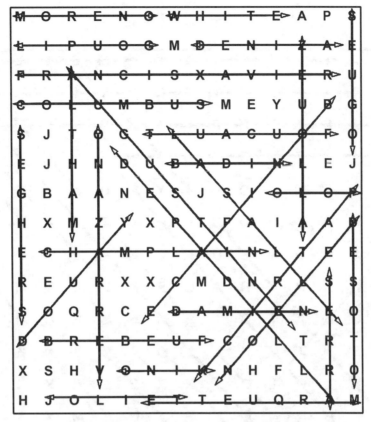

MISSIONARIES & EXPLORERS

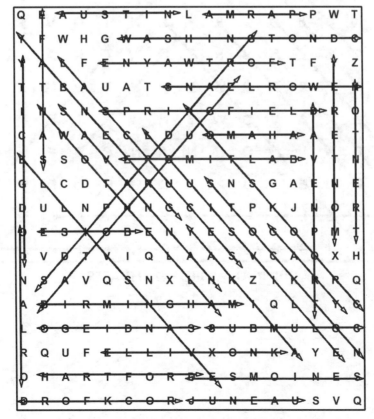

U.S. CITIES WITH CATHEDRALS

WORD SEARCH PUZZLE SOLUTIONS

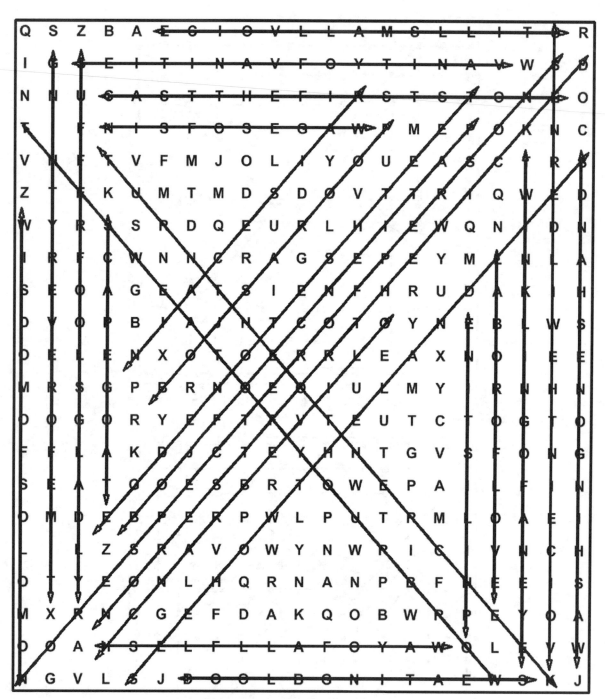

BIBLICAL WORDS & PHRASES

WORD SEARCH PUZZLE SOLUTIONS

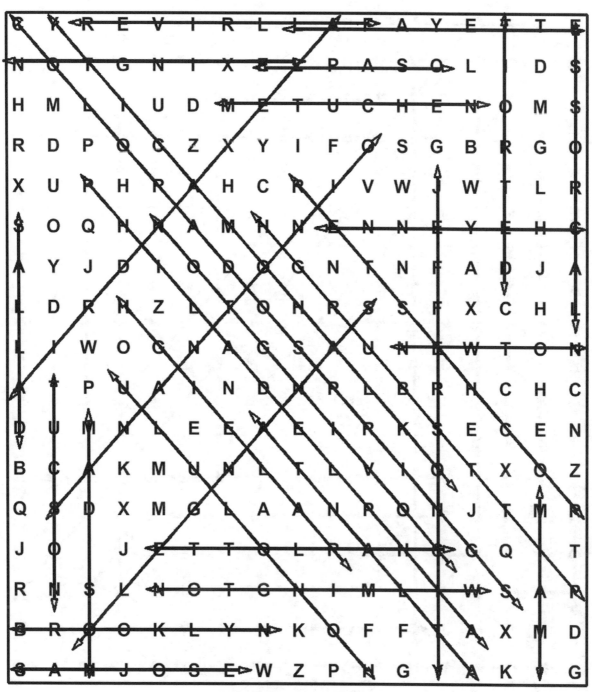

CATHEDRAL CITIES

WORD SEARCH PUZZLE SOLUTIONS

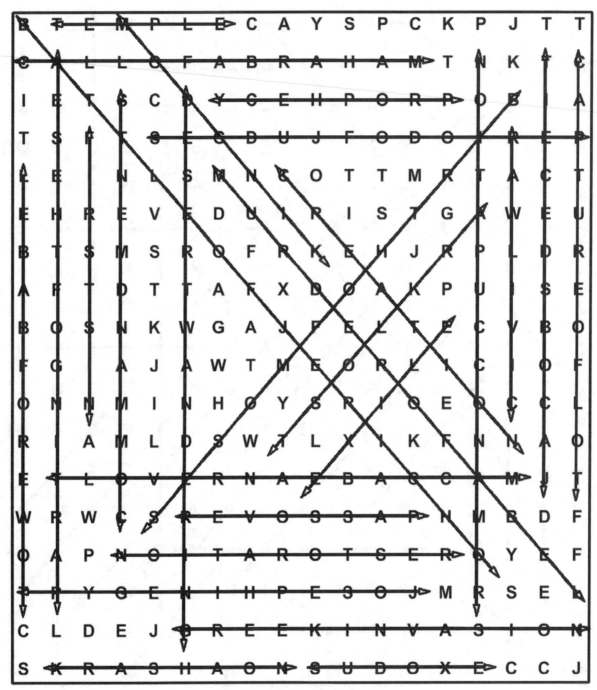

OLD TESTAMENT EVENTS

GAME SOLUTIONS

OLD TESTAMENT BOOKS

1 Song of Solomon
2 Second Maccabees
3 Isaiah
4 Psalms
5 Sirach
6 Genesis
7 Joshua
8 Amos
9 Zechariah
10 First Kings
11 Jeremiah (or Nehemiah)
12 Exodus
13 Ezra
14 Micah
15 First Samuel
16 Esther
17 Baruch
18 Joel
19 Ezekiel
20 Deuteronomy
21 Proverbs
22 Ecclesiastes
23 Habakkuk
24 Leviticus
25 Ruth
26 Job
27 Tobit
28 Malachi
29 Second Samuel
30 Judith
31 Daniel
32 Numbers
33 Second Kings
34 Judges
35 First Chronicles
36 Nehemiah (or Jeremiah)
37 Hosea
38 First Maccabees
39 Jonah
40 Second Chronicles
41 Lamentations
42 Obadiah
43 Nahum
44 Haggai
45 Zephaniah

JUGGLED GEOGRAPHY

1 Jordan River
2 Sea of Galilee
3 Herod's Temple
4 Pool of Bethsaida
5 Garden at Gethsemane
6 Road to Jericho
7 Upper Room
8 Dead Sea
9 Place of the Skull
10 Caesarea Philippi

WORD BUILDER NO. 1
"TRANSCENDENT"

4-Letter Words	5-Letter Words
card	cease
care	crane
cart	crate
cede	creed
dart	dance
dean	dense
dear	eaten
deer	enter
dent	raced
drat	sated
near	scant
neat	scene
need	scent
race	sheer
read	stand
reed	stare
rend	start
sand	state
sate	steed
scan	steer
scar	stent
scat	taste
seat	tease
sect	tense
seed	terse
seer	trace
send	tract
star	trade
tare	tread
tart	treed
tear	treat
teed	trend
tend	
tree	

WHICH IS IT?

He is risen

NUMBERS GAME NO. 1

1 $7+2=9$
2 $+40=49$
3 $-4=45$
4 $-(4 \times 3)=33$
5 $-7=26$
6 $\div 2=13$
7 $-10=3$

3—The number of **persons** in the Trinity

BIBLICAL MENU

Passover (See Ex 12:3–8)

PORTRAITS

1 Abraham
2 John XXIII
3 Solomon
4 Elizabeth
5 John Paul II
6 David
7 Ignatius Loyola
8 Paul
9 Moses
10 Peter

CRYPTOGRAM NO. 1

God is the supreme being who made all things and keeps them in existence.

GAME SOLUTIONS

SAINTS & EMBLEMS

11 Two ravens
9   Ox
1   Lamb
3   Taper
4   Organ
5   Rosary
10 Winged man
12 Sword
13 Tears
6   Cross
7   Keys
15 Arrows
14 Children
2   Shamrock
8   Lion

I CAN NAME THAT ANSWER IN SEVEN CLUES!

I   Thomas Aquinas
II   St. Peter's Basilica
III Canonization
IV   Guadalupe

ACROSTIC

A   Coat
B   Triune
C   Faith
D   Matins
E   Chapel
F   Noon
G   Ciel
H   Home
I   Net

ANSWER: THE NATIONAL SHRINE OF THE IMMACULATE CONCEPTION

ENCYCLICAL MATCH

Humanae Vitae	1968
Mater et Magistra	1961
Ecclesiam Suam	1964
Rerum Novarum	1891
Mysterium Fidei	1965
Populorum Progressio	1967
Redemptor Hominis	1979
Mediator Dei	1947
Divino Afflante Spiritu	1943
Pacem in Terris	1963

WORD BUILDER NO. 2 "RESURRECTION"

4-Letter Words	5-Letter Words
cine	court
cite	crest
coin	crier
cone	crone
core	cruet
corn	crust
cost	curse
cote	cuter
cure	enure
curt	erect
cute	eruct
icon	error
into	ester
iter	inure
nest	nicer
nose	recur
note	recut
rent	reset
rest	resin
rise	reuse
rose	scone
ruse	score
rust	snort
sect	stein
sere	stere
snit	stone
sore	store
sort	surer
sure	terse
tine	toner
tire	
tone	
tore	
unto	
user	

DISTINCTIVE POPES

1   Celestine V
2   Gregory XII
3   John II
4   Marcellus II
5   Adrian IV
6   John Paul II
7   Paul VI
8   Pius X
9   Felix V
10 Leo XIII

JUMBLED WORDS NO. 1

CURATE
ISRAEL
BLESSED
BAPTISM
LITURGY
APOSTLE

Answer: ST. GROUSE'S DAY (the first day of grouse season in England)

JUMBLED WORDS NO. 2

PROPHETS
CHARISM
KNEELER
ETERNITY
EUCHARIST

Answer: THE PEACOCK (its glorious tail is a symbol of the glorified body)

HOLY DAYS OF OBLIGATION

1   Solemnity of Mary, Mother of God
2   Ascension Thursday
3   Feast of the Assumption
4   All Saints Day
5   Feast of the Immaculate Conception
6   Christmas

THE CHRISTMAS QUIZ

Matthew—1, 4, 6
Luke—2, 3, 5

GAME SOLUTIONS

NEW TESTAMENT BOOKS

1 James
2 Romans
3 Philippians
4 Matthew
5 Second Thessalonians
6 Philemon
7 Second Peter
8 Mark
9 Titus
10 Jude (or Luke)
11 Revelation
12 First Peter
13 Luke (or Jude)
14 First Corinthians
15 Colossians
16 First John
17 Galatians
18 John
19 Third John
20 Hebrews
21 Second Timothy
22 Ephesians
23 First Thessalonians
24 Second John
25 First Timothy

PATRON SAINTS

8 Accountants
9 Orators
6 Priests
3 Ecologists
7 Catholic schools
2 Charitable societies
1 Artists
5 Foreign missions
4 Hospitals
10 Youth

CRYPTOGRAM NO. 2

A sacrament is an outward sign instituted by Christ to give grace.

NUMBERS GAME NO. 2

1 12+7=19
2 +40=59
3 −3=56
4 +(7x2)=70
5 −30=40

40—The number of days and nights Moses stayed with God on Mount Sinai

CRYPTOGRAM NO. 3

The theological virtues are faith, hope and charity.

LITURGICAL OBJECTS

3 Ciborium
10 Chalice
8 Monstrance
6 Corporal
4 Ordo
7 Pyx
5 Cruets
2 Aspergillum
9 Censer
1 Amphora

BROTHERS QUIZ

Cain—Abel
Isaac—Ishmael
Esau—Jacob
Ham—Shem
Peter—Andrew
James—John
Joseph—Benjamin
Moses—Aaron

SACRAMENT TEST

SIGN
BAPTISM
RECON**C**ILIATION
CONFI**R**MATION
EUCH**A**RIST
MARRIAGE
HOLY OR**D**ERS
ANOINTI**N**G OF THE SICK
CHRIS**T**

CRYPTOGRAM NO. 4

Hail Mary, full of grace, the Lord is with thee.

HIDDEN BOOKS

1 not **TO BIT**e
2 tall**EST, HER**
3 ho**W IS DOM**inic
4 o**N A HUM**id
5 **JOE L**eft
6 thin**KING, S**hould
7 **HE BREWS**
8 **MARK**
9 **PET ER**ases
10 **GENE SIS**kel

WOMEN OF THE BIBLE

1 Mary Magdalene
2 Esther
3 Miriam
4 Judith
5 Mary
6 Salome
7 Jezebel

JUGGLED SAINTS

Michael the Archangel
Rose of Lima
Teresa of Avila
John Vianney
Catherine of Siena
Peter Claver
Frances Cabrini
Anthony of Padua
Julian of Norwich
Ignatius Loyola
Francis of Assisi
Charles Borromeo
Margaret Mary Alacoque
Joan of Arc
Maxmilian Kolbe

GAME SOLUTIONS

JUGGLED CATHOLIC TERMS

Roman Pontiff
Holy See
Last Judgment
Old Testament
Ten Commandments
Beloved Disciple
Ash Wednesday
Capital Sins
Canon Law
Anno Domini
Divine Office
Ecumenical Council
Feast Days
Sanctifying Grace
Communion Rail

PAPAL MATCH-UP

1 Conclave
2 Pontificate
3 Crossed Keys
4 Chamberlain
5 Encyclical
6 Bull
7 Jesuit
8 Dominican
9 Peter's Pence
10 Castel Gandolfo

CRYPTOGRAM NO. 5

He is going before you to Galilee; there you will see him, as he told you.